BREAKING
Evil
Covenants And Curses

*Unblocking Pathways
That Hinder The Fullness Of God's Blessing*

Paula Matthews

Spirit & Life
Publications^{SM}

BREAKING
Evil Covenants And Curses
*Unblocking Pathways That Hinder
The Fullness Of God's Blessing*
Copyright ©2022 Paula Matthews

All rights reserved.
No part of this book may be
Reproduced in any form by any electronic or
Mechanical means including photocopying,
Recording, or information storage and retrieval
Without written permission from the author.

Unless otherwise noted, scripture quotations
Are from The Holy Bible: King James Version,
©1990 by Thomas Nelson, Inc.

ISBN-13: 978-1-7357642-8-3
Printed in the United States

Spirit & Life
Publications^{SM}
www.spiritandlifepublications.com
Atlanta

AUTHOR'S NOTE

Many of us have been eagerly awaiting for certain prayers to be answered. Why the delay? According to God, many leaders of the Church of Jesus Christ, have been living in a *"spiritual mixture,"* of unholy alliances with the world and with the enemy our souls. Therefore, the Church is out of order. Leaders have led the Lord's flock into rebellion, into thorns and thickets that have choked the word of God from manifesting in their lives.

I recall a young woman moving her family across the country to sit under a man of God, just as the Lord directed her to do. Some time later, she told me that it seemed that God had stopped answering her prayers. She asked me to intercede for her. The Lord revealed that while she had obeyed, the man of God was found in disobedience. One leader's disobedience caused a curse to come upon everyone under his authority. Even his wife was stricken with an illness that would have taken her life, had the man of God not repented.

We, the Body of Christ are *"ordained"* for the Blessing. Yet, when we conform to the world's image instead of that of Jesus Christ, we find ourselves operating under the curse. It's time to return to *holiness*; a total and complete spiritual separation unto God and His will. In times past, God tolerated this so called *"spiritual mixture,"* but not any more. According to the Lord, we are at *"the end of the last days."* We must *"cut off"* all evil alliances and separate from the world system. God is saying to us **"Make no covenant with them** (Deuteronomy 7:2).**"** We have entered into a **New Kingdom Era** and the devil is *"playing a deadly game of keep away"* with our inheritances. We will inherit the promise *if* we don't faint and give in to compromise (Galatians 6:9). If you have found yourself in an evil covenant or curse, be of good cheer, deliverance is at hand. So, get your Bible and follow along with me. Even if you have gone through deliverance in the past, the Lord may have you do it again. Don't argue with God. Obey Him and begin to experience the fullness of His Blessing in this **New Kingdom Era**.

Paula Matthews
Apostle, Prophet
Daughter of the King

CONTENTS

AUTHOR'S NOTE — 5

INTRODUCTION — 11
Jesus Paid For It, We Appropriate It — 11

DEFINING COVENANTS & CURSES — 21
There Is No Curse Without A Cause — 21
God's Purpose For Humanity — 37
Covenants And Consequences — 59

JESUS GAVE US POWER — 79
The Kingdom, Power And Glory Returns — 79
Treading On Serpents And Scorpions — 97
Tearing Down Familial Altars — 113

CONCLUSION — 133
From The Curse To The Blessing — 133
Ruling And Reigning In The Kingdom — 149

PRAYERS — 163
For Deliverance — 163
For Salvation — 164
For Dedication — 165

This Book Is Dedicated To:
The Body Of Christ,
The Church of Jesus Christ
In America And Worldwide

"Places Everyone!"
"God wants the actors center stage . . .
Stay on script no matter what happens . . ."

"The devil will try to distract you with wars,
Rumors of wars, with famine and earthquakes,
With hurricanes and wild fires and economic upheavals,
Pandemics and protests and political rhetoric,
But the show must go on!"

"Instead of saying, 'Break a leg,'
I say to you, 'Break the back of that devil!'"

Excerpt: **The War Journal (2011-2020) Volume III**
The Healing And Restoration of America

INTRODUCTION
Jesus Paid For It, We Appropriate It

God chose us as His covenant people calling us a *"chosen generation, a royal priesthood, and holy nation, a peculiar people* (I Peter 2:9)." Each of us, should be asking ourselves, "Have I chosen Him? Have I chosen God's will as my will?" That same scripture tells us that God chose us for a specific purpose, *"that ye should shew forth the praises of him who hath called you out of darkness into his marvellous light."* Are we really bringing praise and honor to our Father before all the nations of the world? Here is something to consider. Jesus also said that many are called and few are chosen (Matthew 22:14). What does it mean to be chosen? It not only means that God chose us, but that we also chose Him and His will as well. Although God did indeed choose us in Christ before the foundation of the world, He won't force us to choose Him back. We must make the choice to continue in the things of God to become a true disciple of the Lord. *"Then said Jesus to those Jews which believed on him, If ye continue in my word, [then] are ye my disciples indeed; And ye shall know the truth, and the truth shall make you free* (John 8:31-32)."

I must admit that what keeps me motivated to follow after God's will, is my insatiable desire to know truth. I am a "truth seeker." God has separated us to Himself that we might live in truth and in freedom. This is why we get saved; to live a better life than that which the world offers. God shows us something the world cannot offer, the *abundant life* that Jesus came to give us (John 10:10). This is *eternal life*. It's not the life we get after we die. Eternal life begins at salvation. It is the supernatural life of God that flows from His Spirit to ours. That life resides within every believer. Jesus made it available to us, but we must gain knowledge so that we can walk it out by faith. God has given us promises of things that we can have in this *eternal life*. *"According as his divine power hath given unto us all things that [pertain] unto life and godliness, through the knowledge of him that hath called us to glory and virtue: Whereby are given unto us exceeding great and precious promises: that by these ye might be partakers of the divine nature, having escaped the corruption that is in the world through lust* (II Peter 1:3-4)." God has given us everything we need to live abundantly on earth. However, these are things that must be discerned by the spirit. We must *"continue* [abide]*"* in God's word and allow His Spirit to teach us about what is available to us.

"And this is life eternal, that they might know thee the only true God, and Jesus Christ, whom thou hast sent (John 17:3)." It is through *"the knowledge"* of the Father and the Son that we learn of them and what they expect of us. Jesus said, *"Take my yoke upon you, and learn of me; for I am meek and lowly in heart: and ye shall find rest unto your souls. For my yoke is easy, and my burden is light* (Matthew 11:29-30)." There has been much tribulation in the world, as difficult yokes of bondage and heavy burdens have been placed on the people. Still, Jesus by His Spirit is beckoning us to follow His example of how to live holy in a dark and wicked world.

We take His word and learn of His ways. When we follow Him, then we will find rest for our souls. Because His yoke (word) is kind, benevolent towards us and His burden (obligations) are light in comparison to what the world and what religion places on us. The Bible is God's word for our lives. It is to do us good and not evil (Jeremiah 29:11). Tribulation is in the world, but we remain faithful to God. Then what we suffer for Jesus' sake is a *"light affliction,"* when compared to the outcome which includes a glorious reward in the end (II Corinthians 4:17). If anyone ever told you that being a Christian was easy, they lied. Salvation is free, but the way is narrow (Matthew 7:14), and there is much opposition. Read the Bible. Look at what the followers of Jesus suffered. To be *chosen* means to literally "put on" Christ and walk as He walked, even in persecution. Otherwise, we become poor witnesses of what life is like in the Kingdom. Count the cost before signing up for Kingdom service. Anyone can be saved. Walking out your salvation is another story, but that is why God had me write this book.

It takes much strength and courage to be righteous in an unrighteous world. Religion has no power in a world where demonic forces are running rampant. Salvation is about living far above the standards of this world. It requires that we live an uncompromising life in the world, yet we cannot do it alone. We need the Holy Spirit. Zoe is a supernatural life that is *"powered by the Holy Spirit."* Let me explain. The Lord placed a supernatural love in my heart for jet airplanes and sports cars. One day He gave me a *vision* comparing those things with life in Christ. In a *vision*, He showed me what was under the hood of a jet airplane. Then He showed me what was under the hood of a high end sports car. I saw the excellency of the engines, the craftsmanship and attention to detail by those makers. Immediately I got it. God is my Maker! My spirit soared saying, *"I am efficiently fueled and operated, powered by the Holy Ghost!"* That is what it means to be a Christian. *"For we are his workmanship, created in Christ Jesus unto good works, which God hath before ordained that we should walk in them* (Ephesians 2:10)." We are engineered for greatness in this world! Even so, God will not force greatness upon us. It's His will, but it has to be our choice as well. You can quote Ephesians 3:20 all you want, and many Christians do. *"Now unto Him that is able to do exceeding abundantly above all that we ask or think."* We talk about how God *"is able"* but often leave off the key part of that verse. Indeed God is able, but it is *"according to the power that worketh in us."* God cannot do anything in our lives except we enable His power to work through us. This is the resurrection power of the Holy Ghost.

It's takes power to receive what God has in store for us. Jesus walked in power but He didn't walk alone. Neither can we. Jesus was the first to admit, *"I can of mine own self do nothing* (John 5:30)." Jesus also let us know that it was not Him doing the miracles alone. *"The words that I speak unto you I speak not of myself: but the Father that dwelleth in me, he doeth the works* (John 14:10)." Jesus and the Father are one; that means they cooperated one with the other to fulfill God's will. It was Jesus' prayer that we operate the same. *"And the glory which thou gavest me I have given them; that they may be one, even as we are one: I in them, and thou in me, that they may be made perfect in one; and that the world may know that thou hast sent me, and hast loved them, as thou hast loved me* (John 17:22-23)."

Jesus never operated in life alone. He needed the Holy Ghost in order to perform the will of His Father. It's no different for the believer. If we continue in His word then we will be **"efficiently fueled."** If we follow the Holy Ghost, we will be **"efficiently operated."** We are engineered to be **"powered"** by the Holy Spirit. Think about your automobile. If you want the optimum performance, you can't just put any fuel in the tank. You can't even do that with lawn equipment. Each engine type requires a specific kind of fuel mixture. One must follow the manufacturer's instructions for efficient operation. We understand these things when it comes to operating vehicles and equipment, but not so much when we are operating in God's Kingdom. Yet, it's the same principle at work.

Think about this. It takes faith to receive the promises of God. Faith is the *"substance of things hoped for, the evidence of things not seen* (Hebrews 11:1)." Before we can have hope for something from God, we must see it with our spiritual **"eyes of faith."** That is why it is necessary to read the Bible. Not only must we see it written, but we must believe what we are reading. That Bible gives us *"evidence"* of what God has promised. You may not see that thing in the physical realm, but the promise of that thing does exist according to the Bible. God will also show us things in visions and dreams by His Holy Spirit. These things are also *"evidence,"* of things to hope for. Whatever God shows us, He is sure to give instruction on how to obtain, what we have been shown. God is able to do exceeding abundantly, but if we don't believe (have faith) in what God is showing (telling) us, we won't see it manifested in our lives. That's why the writer of Hebrews said that *"without faith"* it is impossible to please God (Hebrews 11:6). God is not pleased when we don't believe what He tells us. What then, is the purpose of calling yourself a believer, when you don't really believe?

The Bible says that if we come to God asking anything, we must believe *"that He is"* what He says He is, and that He will do what He says He will do (Hebrews 11:6). We must also believe that God *"is rewarder of those who diligently seek Him."* If you want what God has for your life, you must diligently seek after Him. God loved us so much that He sacrificed His Son. Jesus paid for our redemption with His Blood, but that was not the end of the story. If we believe that God loves us, then we respond to His love by diligently seeking to appropriate everything that has been given to us. The Apostle Paul says it this way, *"But I follow after, if that I may apprehend that for which also I am apprehended of Christ Jesus* (Philippians 3:12)."

The Lord gave me a *vision* of how salvation is suppose to work. *In the realm of the spirit there appeared a humongous credit card with the name Jesus Christ written on it. Imagine a card in His Name. The Lord explained that as a believer, I was an authorized user of His credit card. Every time I would ask for a specific promise of God for my life, the Lord would show that it was like that credit card was being swiped by a credit card reader. To make it very clear, each time I swiped the card, I heard a "cha-ching" of a cash register box in the spirit. The Lord gave me John 14:14 to explain what was going on in this vision. "If you shall ask anything in my name, I will do it."* In other words, if it's on the card [in the Bible], I can ask for it and He will do it. Why? Because it's already paid for. It's in the account awaiting our requisition. We have to use the card, if we want to receive what is rightfully ours by covenant. The currency we use is our faith. We have to believe what Jesus did for us. We also must believe that we can, and will receive it. However, if we don't ask, we won't receive, even though Jesus paid for it all.

I recently noticed how many times Jesus told us to *"ask"* for what we want in the Book of John. Jesus was attempting to explain to His disciples the relationship they would have with the Father, after He was crucified and resurrected. Up until then, Jesus, the Master, Healer, Miracle worker was all that they knew. He chose them and gave them His example to follow. When they asked Jesus to *"Shew us the Father."* Jesus said, *"He that hath seen me hath seen the Father* (John 14:9)." Stop! This ought to be the goal of every believer. When people see us, they should see the Father. How could this be? Jesus makes it quite simple. He said, when He spoke God's word, the Father did the work (John 14:10). The same is true of every believer. Jesus said, *"Verily, verily, I say unto you, He that believeth on me, the works that I do shall he do also; and greater works than these shall he do; because I go unto my Father* (John 14:12)." Manifesting these greater works is why God has chosen us. When we cease from doing our own works it allows the Father to work through us. Jesus continued by saying, *"And whatsoever ye shall ask in my name, that I will do, that the Father may be glorified in the Son* (John 14:13)."

Jesus was preparing his disciples for His departure, preparing their hearts and teaching them how to do what He did. Jesus has left the earth, but His word is here in His stead. We can ask the Father, He will give us another Comforter, to abide with us forever, even the Spirit of Truth (John 14:16-17). Notice, that Jesus is not telling us to ask Him. Jesus told us to ask of the Father. That's what Jesus did when He walked this earth. Then Jesus describes the relationship between the believer, the Father and the Son. If we *"abide"* in Him, then we are one with Him. *"If ye abide in me, and my words abide in you, ye shall ask what ye will, and it shall be done unto you* (John 15:7)." Asking *"anything"* requires that we are abiding in Him. Going back to the credit card example. If what I desire is against the will of God, I can ask and swipe the card all day long and that transaction will be rejected. The Bible says, *"And this is the confidence that we have in him, that if we ask anything according to his will, he heareth us: and if we know that he hear us, whatsoever we ask, we know that we have the petitions that we desire of him* (I John 5:14-15)." Whatever we ask, we receive of him because we keep his commandments and do those things that are pleasing in his sight (I John 3:22). In short, we must do what is pleasing to God, or we won't receive from Him. This is covenant talk. Things have been set aside for our benefit, but we have to be in right position with God in order to receive. It's all paid for, but we must do what is necessary to receive. Salvation means that we are reconciled back to God and His purpose for our lives. At salvation we become *"new"* creatures with a *"new"* purpose for living, and that purpose is God. Jesus said, *"Ye have not chosen me, but I have chosen you, and ordained you, that ye should go and bring forth fruit, and that your fruit should remain: that whatsoever ye shall ask of the Father in my name, he may give it you (John 15:16)."* Jesus is saying that we were chosen and ordained to ask of God in His name [His will and purpose], just so the Father may give it to us. How easy is that? You've heard of the term "born to shop." We were **"born again to ask and receive."** Each time we do, it's like the swiping that credit card. Only, we shop with the Father's card to purchase what He has already laid up for us. Again, Jesus said in John 16:23, *"And in that day, ye shall ask me nothing. Verily, verily, I say unto you, Whatsoever ye shall ask the Father in my name, he will give it you."* Notice how in His absence, Jesus is granting us direct access to the Father so that we can fulfill what is required in our divine purpose. This is how a covenant works. Each party has to fulfill their part of the agreement in order to enjoy the benefits of the covenant.

Jesus completed His work through His death and resurrection. He made all power available to us, both that which is in heaven and in earth. Then He told us to go in His Name (Matthew 28:18-19). After the resurrection, God the Father, set Jesus at his own right hand in the heavenly places, far above all principality, and power, and might, and dominion, and every name that is named, not only in this world, but also in that which is to come. When we received Jesus as our Lord, God also raised us up together with Christ and made us to sit together in heavenly places with Him (Ephesians 1:20-21; 2:5-6). This is what I saw with the credit card. All power was given to the believer, just as it was given to Jesus, except our power rests in His Name. When I made a purchase with that card, it was as though Jesus made the purchase Himself. It was like believers are the **"silent partners** (agents of God)" in the realm of the spirit. On earth, people see us, but in Heaven God sees Jesus. The assignment, the knowledge, the faith and the power is of God, not of us.

In light of this, I must share a *real life incident* in which I almost died because of a hesitancy to appropriate the word that the Holy Spirit gave me to speak. I will never forget that night as long as I live. Something evil had come over me and I could not shake it. At one single moment in the spirit, I saw the faces of every person who ever hated me, all praying for my demise, at the same time. This was not natural. It was a supernatural plot against my life. I prayed and asked the Lord what was going on. The answer He gave was not what I wanted to hear. He said that **"the principality over this city wants you dead tonight."** Well, I knew that the Lord had sent me to that city on assignment. So, I responded, "I know you're not telling me this because you want me dead. What shall I do?" The Lord quoted II Chronicles 7:14. *"If my people, which are called by my name, shall humble themselves, and pray, and seek my face, and turn from their wicked ways; then will I hear from heaven, and will forgive their sin, and will heal their land."* I responded in pride, "What have I done that I need to repent?" Then the Lord then said something too crazy to believe. He said, **"Repent for the sins of your fathers."** Instead of obeying, I began to argue with the Lord. "What?" "Why do I have to repent for something they did?" I began quoting scripture about Jesus being made a curse for me. I told God that Jesus had paid for all my sins. It didn't make sense that I repent for what my parents did. It was also stupid of me to argue Bible scriptures with the God who wrote the Bible, but that's exactly what I did. Then, God said one word that made me shut my mouth. He said to me, **"You're the one who is dying. Are you going to do what I say, or die fighting me?"** He was right, the more I argued, the weaker my body became. So, I stopped arguing and repented. "Lord, I repent for the sins of my fathers." IMMEDIATELY, my body was healed and I was back to normal.

Consider what could have happened had I not asked what I should do. What if I had began going after that principality? What if I had stood upon scriptures like Isaiah 53:5, saying "With Jesus' stripes I am healed?" What if I had repeatedly quoted Isaiah 54:17, *"No weapon formed against me shall prosper."* These are good scriptures, but inappropriate for that situation. Listen, knowing scripture is wonderful. Knowing how and when to use scripture is **"efficient and effectual."** The Bible says to get wisdom, which is the word of God, but it also tells us to *"get understanding* (Proverbs 4:7)." Once I got understanding I immediately obeyed. There should have been an understanding from the beginning that God was the boss; that He knew more than I did. Somehow, my perceived knowledge of scripture was my defense. But, God knew how to break through my pride. He knew just the words to get my attention. He broke it down clean and simple, **"You're the one who is dying..."** One simple word from the Spirit of God immediately delivered me out of my pride and out of a deadly situation. It wouldn't have mattered that I was seated together with Jesus, if I didn't have access to that power. I wasn't in position to receive power, until I repented. The Bible says, *"As He is, so are we in this world* (I John 4:17)." In reflection, I needed to reconsider my position. How was Jesus at that moment? How was I at that same moment? Jesus and I were not *"one"* in that moment. Until I submitted to God, I had no power to resist the devil that wanted me dead that night (James 4:7). God was able, but I had to be willing and obedient. The power came in my repentance. For deliverance to go forth, I had to speak the words the Father gave me. When I spoke what the Father said, He was able to do the work. I don't ever want to take the voice of the Father for granted. In that incident, there was time to recover. It only concerned my life. God forbid that it be about the lives of loved ones or others whom the Lord entrusted to my care. I want to always be *"willing and obedient"* to obey the voice of the Lord. Although God will give us things because it's His word, I want to obey from the heart, out of love for the Father who has been so very good to me.

I'm sensing in my spirit that I need to stay on this point for a moment. We have been taught as Christians that God loved the world so much that He sent His son to die for us. *"For God so loved the world, that he gave his only begotten Son, that whosoever believeth in him should not perish, but have everlasting life* (John 3:16)." It is very important to get saved and not to perish. It is also very important to receive the eternal life, but I am sensing in my spirit something more. There is a **"precedent"** that has been set before us. It's a **"precedent of love."** God so loved us that He sent Jesus to the earth to show us how to love. How did Jesus love? He walked in the love and honor of the Father. *"If ye keep my commandments, ye shall abide in my love; even as I have kept my Father's commandments, and abide in his love* (John 15:10)." This is all that the Father desires from us; that we abide in His love. We abide by keeping (obeying) His word; by doing whatever His Spirit instructs us to do.

When I look back on that night when the principality struck me, I am humbled, even as I write this chapter. Jesus paid for my high calling with His Blood. Prior to that night, I had been abiding in the love of God. The Lord had given me so much revelation. I had numerous trips to Heaven and came back with knowledge about these last days before Jesus returns. Looking back, I see how easy it is for the flesh to rise up against God. I was in the presence of God in Heaven when He answered all the questions of my heart and I never had to speak a word. He showed me things about His creation that I had never known. He showed me the timeline of history of the world and the return of His Son, and yet I had the audacity to argue with the Source of all the knowledge that I had gained. There was obviously something within me that needed to be **"uprooted."** And, I submit to you that as long as we are in this body made of flesh, something within us will need to be **"rooted out."** I could have made the choice not to live and forfeit all the promises of God for my life. Sure, I would have gone to heaven, but I would have not enjoyed all the benefits of my salvation in this life. I made up my mind to do all that is necessary to receive everything that Jesus died and resurrected to restore back to me. Yes, you heard correctly. I said "restore." Salvation is about *restoration*. It's about restoring mankind back to God's original plan and destiny for our lives.

Consider where we would be if Adam had never sinned. Every human being on earth would be living a righteous life today. Think about it. If sin had never happened, we would have been living life in God's marvelous Light from the time we were born and for all eternity. We would have been enjoying all the wealth and provision Heaven could supply upon this earth. That was God's original plan for His kids. Sin caused the plan to be somewhat altered, but the outcome will be the same. Jesus paid for our restoration as the righteous sons and daughters of the Most High God. Don't just think salvation is about dying and going to Heaven. It's much more than that. It's about God restoring this earth as His Kingdom both in power and in glory, through His kids, for all who believe.

None of this happens automatically. We have to do our part. According to the Lord, in these last days, if we want to obtain the promises, we have to work at entering into His rest (Hebrews 4:10). We cannot continue doing what we believe is right. God is the righteous Judge. When the Lord told me that the devil is **"playing a deadly game of keep away"** with our inheritances, I was determined to get mine at whatever cost. We are in a New Kingdom Era in which God desires to save millions and billions of souls in order to give them an inheritance. The devil wants to eliminate as many people as he can before people can receive. We need not worry about what the devil is doing. We need to get serious with God. We need to get into position, in that secret place of the Most High so that we can learn about all that the Father has ordained for our lives. I found out first hand that our protection is in our obedience. The enemy will continue devising wars, famines, pestilences and the like, but we have **"diplomatic immuni-**

ty," because we are not from here. We are citizens of the Kingdom of God. Those who know their God will be strong and do exploits (Daniel 11:32). One of the characteristics of this New Kingdom Era will be saints of God who know their god-given rights and exercise them with boldness. We will possess the land. Gone are the days of the **"weak wimpy can't help myself"** Christian. This is do, or die in the wilderness. We are in the final season of earth before Jesus returns. He is coming back for *"a glorious Church, not having spot, or wrinkle, or any such thing; but that it should be holy and without blemish* (Ephesians 5:27)." This is our **"final call"** to rededicate ourselves to the plan and purpose of God. This call is for the saved and unsaved alike.

According to God, humanity is in a similar place where the Children of Israel were after they were released from slavery in Egypt. God delivered them with a *"mighty hand and an outstretched arm* (Deuteronomy 26:8)." Then He had to form a nation from those who had been enslaved for over four hundred years. Likewise, God is restoring a Kingdom in the earth with those who have been enslaved to a world system. All we have ever known is this world system, but God is tearing it down. The only refuge will be in God's Kingdom. Therefore, we must inherit the land and walk in His ways. We have no choice if we are to survive what is coming upon the earth. God will be coming down hard upon all unrighteousness. He wants to make sure that His Children are not harmed. At the same time, He wants us to inherit what is rightfully ours in this final season before Jesus returns. God is requiring that we completely sever all ties with the works of darkness. For most of us, it begins with breaking evil covenants and curses that have plagued our lives for multiple generations since the time of Adam.

DEFINING COVENANTS & CURSES

There Is No Curse Without A Cause

People in the world are familiar with curses. Few are as familiar with the Blessing that God pronounced on mankind. *"And God blessed them, and God said unto them, Be fruitful, and multiply, and replenish the earth, and subdue it: and have dominion over the fish of the sea, and over the fowl of the air, and over every living thing that moveth upon the earth (Genesis 1:28)."* The Blessing was what God placed upon mankind as an endowment. The curse was man's choice. It brought results that were quite opposite to the Blessing. It would seem that people have been conditioned to receive the curse rather than the Blessing. In fact, much of American media is centered around witchcraft and curses. It is portrayed in our books, movies and film as a form of entertainment. Unfortunately, the only one not talking about curses is the Church. Instinctively people can sense that things are not right in the world, but is it a curse? They want to be happy but happiness alludes them. They obtain wealth and it's either stolen or it slips through their hands. They desire peace but none is to be found. They are suffering from wars, famine, sickness and disease. People long to be safe and secure but it cannot be found in this world. What is found, never lasts. These are the signs of a curse. *To be cursed, means to be empowered or destined to fail.*

Many Christians suffer under the curse like those who don't know God. The world blames God for the cursed conditions of mankind. Yet according to scripture, mankind chose the curse. It began when Adam sinned in the Garden of Eden. Sin brought the curse in Adam's day. It still brings the curse in our day. The curse results from spiritual laws that reside on earth. To understand covenants and curses we must discuss how God created the earth. Covenants and curses were originally God's ideas. Whatever God creates is for a specific purpose. The same is true for the covenant and the curse. When God created the heavens and the earth, it all was designed to be upheld by the power of His word [God's laws] for all eternity. *"While the earth remaineth, seedtime and harvest, and cold and heat and summer and winter, and day and night shall not cease (Genesis 8:22)."* God established natural laws that regulate time, space and matter on earth. One such law is the law of gravity which ensures that matter remains grounded upon the earth. Whether natural or spiritual, the laws that God established never change. Neither can they be changed except by God Himself. Mankind has attempted to regulate times and seasons for his own convenience, but they can only do so within the constraints of God's established law. Seedtime and harvest is the law that we will concentrate on for our discussion. This is a law that establishes the consequences of the actions and responses of both mankind and nature upon the earth.

When God created man and put him in the garden, he was given laws of conduct. We call them *"commandments."* The Bible says, *"And the Lord God took the man, and put him into the garden of Eden to dress it and to keep it. And the Lord God commanded the man, saying, Of every tree of the garden thou mayest freely eat: but of the tree of the knowledge of good and evil, thou shalt not eat of it: for in the day that thou eatest thereof thou shalt surely die* (Genesis 2:15-17)." Notice how God put the man in the garden and gave him an assignment. The man was expected to cultivate the garden. He quickly became a manager over God's business interest. Surely, God gave the man instructions on how to work the garden. Adam learned what would be expected of him in that assignment. He also was told what to avoid. God freely gave the man access to eat from every tree in the garden, except for one, the tree of the knowledge of good and evil. This was not an suggestion. This was a commandment. It was the law in the garden. God let the man know that the penalty for breaking that law, was death.

God commanded the man and gave the consequences of his disobedience. Unfortunately, Adam didn't understand what it meant to die. Therefore, he had no fear of death like many have today. We know what it means to die and try to avoid it at any cost. Some might say that the greatest fear of mankind is the fear of death. It wasn't the case in Adam's day. There was no fear. There was no death in the garden. It will be that way again some day. *"And God shall wipe away all tears from their eyes; and there shall be no more death, neither sorrow, nor crying, neither shall there be any more pain: for the former things are passed away* (Revelation 21:4)." The Bible says that there is coming a new heaven and a new earth, but we don't have to wait. We can get a glimpse of that new earth in God's Kingdom right now. Sin brought death into the world. It is the curse. However, that's not the end of the story. Jesus restored the Blessing to us. We now have a choice to choose the Blessing. *"I call heaven and earth to record this day against you, that I have set before you life and death, blessing and cursing: therefore choose life that both thou and thy seed may live* (Deuteronomy 30:19)." It's God's desire that we would live in the Blessing. Yet, the choice is ours.

God gave mankind dominion in the earth. Which means God won't make a life or death choice for us. That might surprise some people because we have heard it said, *"And said, Naked came I out of my mother's womb, and naked shall I return thither: the LORD gave, and the LORD hath taken away; blessed be the name of the LORD (Job 1:21)."* Remember the story of Job? Did the Lord really take away the mans wealth and kill his children? No! According to the Bible, it was the man's fear that brought the destruction upon him. Job said, *"For the thing which I greatly feared is come upon me, and that which I was afraid of is come unto me (Job 3:25)."* Job was so fearful that something bad was going to happen, that he brought it upon himself.

God created us to give us a Blessed life on earth. He doesn't kill. The Bible says, *"As the bird by wandering, as the swallow by flying, so the curse causeless shall not come (Proverbs 26:2)."* Death and loss are the consequences of this cursed system in the earth. When Adam chose to turn away from God, he chose the curse for all of mankind. One man's sin brought death upon us all. Even so, God's grace towards mankind, has restored to us the choice of life and the Blessing through His covenant [agreement] with Jesus Christ. We have no excuse. Where we stand with God will either invoke the Blessing or the curse. The choice is ours. If we choose to obey God we will have life and the Blessing. If we choose to disobey God we will have death and the curse. God will not force us to obey His law. However, the consequences of our choices will be made manifest in our lives, in the lives of our children and in our children's children. In any case, it should be noted that both the curse and the Blessing must have a cause. Obedience to God results in the Blessing. Disobedience results in sin and the curse.

There is good news for chose who are experiencing the curse. You don't have to stay there. Whether you are saved or not, the curse is a reality of life, but it's not the final answer. *"For as by one man's disobedience many were made sinners, so by the obedience of one shall many be made righteous (Roman 5:19)."* In this scripture the Apostle Paul gives the cause of both the Blessing and the curse. Adam's disobedience resulted in all of mankind being born into sin. This scripture also says that by one man's obedience, meaning Jesus' obedience that led to His death on the cross, many people will be made righteous. Notice how Adam's curse took away our choice. All of us were born into sin. We didn't have a choice, but to be cursed in this world. But thanks be to God for His mercy and grace towards us. He sent Jesus to show us the way back to the Blessing in this earth. However, the curse was not eradicated. The curse was made manifest by the law of sin and death. Salvation initiates another law that overrides the curse. *"For the law of the Spirit of life in Christ Jesus hath made me free from the law of sin and death* (Romans 8:2).*"* In Christ, we have a way out of the curse. Salvation does not change the world. It changes individuals who affect change in the world. The systems of the world were cursed at their foundation since most were established in defiance of God's commandments. *"Thus saith the LORD; Cursed [be] the man that trusteth in man, and maketh flesh his arm, and whose heart departeth from the LORD* (Jeremiah 17:5).*"* World systems are destined to fall. History records the rise and fall of many kingdoms, nations and lands that are not with us today. This was by divine purpose.

God established the foundations of this earth by His word. His word is eternal. God's word is timeless. It never changes. Whatever God commands, becomes law upon the earth. Mankind has chosen to create world governments that oppose God's law. They shall not stand. The law of seedtime and harvest is in effect. World governments will always reap whatever they have sown (Galatians 6:7). If they sow seeds of discord, harm, and anger towards others to gain power and dominance, the same will manifest in that nation. It's a simple concept that men choose not to remember. *"And as ye would that men should do to you, do ye also to them likewise."* The law of seedtime and harvest is immutable. It can never change. It is the pattern of life in the earth. The pattern of death is no different. *"For he that soweth to his flesh shall of the flesh reap corruption; but he that soweth to the Spirit shall of the Spirit reap life everlasting* (Galatians 6:8).*"* Sowing to the flesh means sowing seeds out of hurt or out of our feelings, emotions or intellect. This scripture says that if anyone sows seeds other than what God ordained, they will ultimately reap death. That is exactly what happened to Adam. He turned way from obeying God to obeying his human instinct and desire. This led to a separation from God and ultimately to the death and curse upon all mankind.

I feel led to share a prophetic *vision* the Lord gave me some years ago, that demonstrates the Blessing and the curse.[1] *In this vision, it seemed like two video tracks were playing, maybe even a double vision in which I saw two scenarios playing at the same time. In each scenario there was a single train running on a track. Each train was carrying a specific group of people. Each track represented a way of being and living in this life. On one track, I saw a train*

---

1   Matthews, Paula. "A Missed Opportunity Leaves An Ace In The Hole." *The War Journal (2011-2020) Volume 3.* Atlanta: Spirit & Life Publications℠, 2020. 61-64 . Print.

*carrying people operating as the world does, everyone doing their own thing. They were following the ways of what they heard in the media or what they had seen their families do, or what the culture was telling them. They were on the train on the track of everyday life. On the other track, I saw a train carrying people who were hearing the voice of God operating based upon what God was saying. These people did what God told them to do. They spoke what God spoke. I heard God speaking things, and things happened. I heard God telling things to move, and things moved. He said, **"Let there be . . ."** And, whatever He called by name, came forth. It happened. I heard God speak abundance. Abundance came forth. I heard God speak health and deliverance. Health and deliverance came forth in the earth. All of this happened on this one train track which God called **"Life And Abundance."***

*God called the other track, **"Everyday Life In America."** People were shooting. They were killing. They were deceiving. The Word of God was being preached, but no one on that train was listening. They were just going on with life as usual in America. Then the Lord showed that down the track was something that looked like a stone wall. This same stone wall appeared to be on both tracks on which either train ran. It was not only on both tracks, but also at the same location and position on each track. However something was different about how that stone wall appeared. On the track called, **"Everyday Life In America"** no one seemed to notice that the stone wall had no opening. The train was moving at a fast pace and was about to hit this wall. On the other track called, **"Life And Abundance,"** the train was moving rapidly to the same spot on its track, but there was an opening in the stone wall. There appeared a tunnel that allowed the train to pass straight-through in safety.*

Here is how the Holy Spirit explained this vision. He said that the stone wall, is Jesus Christ. To those who believe, He is precious, but to those who choose disobedience, Jesus is *"a stone of stumbling and a rock of offence* (I Peter 2:7-8)." People in America, even in the Church, are offended by Jesus because they don't want to change how they live. Regardless of their views on life, the train of **"Everyday Life In America"** was headed for destruction. Those on board are people who live according to what they see, how they feel or how they think. In their minds, they believe their way is right. The Bible says, *"There is a way which seemeth right unto a man, but the end thereof [are] the ways of death* (Proverbs 14:12)." Indeed that was the case for the train of **"Everyday Life In America."** People did what was right in their own eyes and it led to a train wreck. That train had no choice but to crash into the very *Rock* that offended them. The train on the track of *"Everyday Life In America"* hit the stonewall and derailed sharply. Everyone on this train died. The other train on the track of *"Life And Abundance,"* passed through the stonewall because there was an opening its side of the track. All of its passengers were safe. Notice how God only described only two paths in this life. We are either with Him, or against Him. There is no such thing as "doing our own thing" in God's green earth. There is no middle ground with Him. Even Christians grapple at this. They want to go to Heaven, but only if they can live anyway they choose in this life. Since those who are on the track of *"Life And Abundance,"* have received Jesus and obey Him, they will go through this life with God's Grace. They will prosper and flourish even in times of trouble, because they believe God. The Lord sent His Word *"to save the world from destruction* (Psalm 107:20)." Few are listening.

In America, most people are not trying to get on the track that leads to life, because they don't see the value in it. Neither do they see the stone wall set before them that will alter the course of their lives and destinies for all eternity. Unfortunately, no one can see the truth of God's plan for their lives, unless they come to Him. They must be *"born again"* to be able to see the things of the Kingdom (John 3:3). So, what is God saying will happen in America? The Lord says, *"It is time for the crash."* There is no way of stopping the train. It will crash and very soon. The only option is for people to hear the truth and deboard the train of *"Everyday Life In America."* Jesus came to give us life, but we have a choice to make. If we want life, then we must choose life.

How does one choose life? The same way we choose death, by the words of our mouths. The Bible says, *"Death and life [are] in the power of the tongue: and they that love it shall eat the fruit thereof* (Proverbs 18:21)." If you enjoy speaking evil things, then evil is what you will get in your life. People curse themselves by the words that they speak over themselves and others. Remember that the law of seedtime and harvest is working in the earth. If you want life and the Blessing then choose the words that will bring those things forth in your life. What are those words? Jesus told us in John 6:63. *"The words that I speak unto you, they are spirit, and they are life."* Peter said that Jesus had *"the words of eternal life* (John 6:68)." The word of God brings life; to Bless and not curse us. Now, there are curses mentioned in the Bible. They are *"deterrents"* that show us what evils are lurk in the darkness ready to prey upon those who disobey God's law. The curse is definitely in the earth, but that does not mean we have to live under its mandates. God has done everything in His power to provide a way for us to experience His best in this earth. Evil things may be happening all around us, but they will not touch those who are following the Lord. They are **"exempt"** from the curses of the world. *"A thousand shall fall at thy side, and ten thousand at thy right hand; but it shall not come nigh thee. Only with thine eyes shall thou behold and see the reward of the wicked . . . There shall no evil befall thee, neither shall any plague come nigh thy dwelling.* (Psalm 91:7-10)." The righteous are protected under the shadow of God's wings. However, evil <u>will</u> befall [come upon] the wicked.

Please understand that "wicked" does not necessarily mean evil. Wicked simply means "skewed" or "twisted," in ones understanding and behavior. Sometimes this happens out of ignorance. People just don't know they are doing wrong. That does not **"exempt"** them from the consequences of their actions. Innocent people are often hurt because of the curse. There are children who are sick and dying because of the choices their parents made. Children don't have a choice, but adults do. There are people in nations at war, dying because of choices their leaders have made. Jesus said they be *"blind leaders of the blind"* and they both will fall into the ditch (Matthew 15:14). Ignorance of God's law does not **"exempt"** you from the consequences of said law. In fact, God says, *"My people are destroyed for lack of knowledge* (Hosea 4:6)." Yet, so many Christians reject the knowledge that God wants to impart to them. They would rather take the word of a man over the word of God. They would rather follow the ways of men that seem right, rather than following the instruction of the Lord that will always work in their favor. The Blessing is enjoyed by those who know that God has our backs, no matter what comes our way. He alone will deliver us.

Unfortunately, so many of God's people no longer trust God. They say they do, but their actions prove otherwise. They are actually operating with a *"evil heart of unbelief."* The writer of Hebrews warns us. *"Take heed, brethren, lest there be in any of you an evil heart of unbelief, in departing from the living God* (Hebrews 3:12)." The Bible calls *"unbelief"* <u>evil</u>. Those are strong words, but that is how God sees things when His people refuse to believe His word. Many are living compromised lives and say, "God knows my heart." Sure He does. As the Bible says, *"The heart is deceitful above all things, and desperately wicked: who can know it?"* Then God answers that question saying, *"I the Lord search the heart, I try the reins, even to give every man according to his ways, and according to the fruit of his doings (Jeremiah 17:9-10)."* In other words, every person will reap what he or she sows. Listen, God knows the hearts of saints and sinners alike. Sinners sin. That's what they do. Wicked people do wickedness. Oh, Christians do not do as they do. Obey God. Don't feel pressured to follow the ways of unbelievers. Seek God for answers on how to navigate through the curse of this world. *"There hath no temptation taken you but such as is common to man: but God [is] faithful, who will not suffer you to be tempted above that ye are able; but will with the temptation also make a way to escape, that ye may be able to bear [it] (I Corinthians 10:13)."* If God has the answer, if He has the *"way to escape"* then all we need do is ask and receive the answer that we need in each and every situation. There is no reason that Christians should be in unbelief.

The bottom line is this. What God has Blessed, no man can curse (Numbers 23:8). However, we can curse ourselves, and often do. I exhort you to do as God suggested in Deuteronomy 30:19, *"choose life"* so that you and your children may live. Sure the devil wants you to remain in the curse, but God wants you Blessed. God will even protect the Blessing on your life and multiply it to others. *"I will bless them that bless thee, and curse him that curseth thee (Genesis 12:3)."* On the other hand, God promises to curse those who put curses on you. Want to curse yourself? Then curse another person. The seed you sowed will spring forth a harvest in your own life. Still, turning our hearts back to God makes us **"exempt"** from the curse. Indeed, what God Blesses cannot, and will not be cursed. Even if we choose to walk the way of the curse, the Blessing is not removed. It's may not be **"activated"** in our lives, but it's not removed.

Think about this. From the very beginning, everything God created was "Blessed." It met God's seal of approval. *"And God saw everything that he had made, and behold it was very good (Genesis 1:31)."* What God created was designed to remain on the earth forever. This is eternal life, God's *"eternal"* purpose for mankind. We were never created to die, yet sinful men certainly die under the curse. God sent Jesus into the world to restore the Blessing to all of mankind. *"Christ hath redeemed us from the curse of the law, being made a curse for us: for it is written, Cursed [is] every one that hangeth on a tree: That the blessing of Abraham might come on the Gentiles through Jesus Christ; that we might receive the promise of the Spirit through faith* (Galatians 3:13-14)." Jesus came to restore God's Blessing to mankind. This is the reason for salvation. It's not about going to Heaven. It's about bringing days of Heaven back upon the earth (Deuteronomy 11:21). Don't just take my word for it. Get your Bible. Read the scriptures. Commit this matter to the Lord in prayer. He will answer you if you seek Him with an earnest heart. The Blessing is available to all who will seek and obey God.

Talk like this is difficult for many to hear because generations of preachers have been preaching about Heaven and hell. Now, Heaven is a real place. So is hell, but Jesus never taught about either. Sure, He mentioned them, but Jesus only taught the Kingdom of God. He taught His followers how to navigate this cursed world with the Blessing. The Gospel of the Kingdom is about destroying the works of the devil (the curse), and walking in the Blessing. Preaching against sin never stopped people from sinning. In fact, it seemed like people just found *"more creative ways to sin within the law."* They missed the whole purpose for salvation. If salvation was about going to Heaven, then God would immediately take us all right after we got saved. That did not happen. God has a greater purpose for our salvation. I recall the Lord telling me, *"I didn't save you for yourself."* I was happy to know I was going to Heaven, but God wanted more from me. People around me were suffering. They were talking about their sicknesses, about who was dead or dying. They claimed Jesus as their Savior, but were giving praise to satan by saying, "The devil is busy." They claimed faith in God, yet they had no testimony to His goodness in their lives other than, "God woke me up this morning." Sure He did, but they had the same sickness, the same poverty, and the same complaints as those in the world. They were giving no glory to God. Why wouldn't they say, "God is busy?" What do they think the God of the Bible was doing while the devil was busy? Again, the curse comes because of the words we speak over the situations of our lives.

The Bible says that the Blessing of the Lord makes rich and He adds no sorrow with it (Proverbs 10:22). If we are indeed Blessed of the Lord, we should have no sorrow. Yet, too many Christians are confessing sorrow and attributing it all to God's way of teaching them a lesson. Pain and sorrow is not from God. It is part of the curse that is in the world. The curse cannot come upon us without our permission. As we said before, the curse comes upon us because we've departed from God (Jeremiah 17:5). He does not leave us. We leave Him and His word. Let me share an example. I am an American citizen by birth. As Americans, we like the freedom to do our own thing. People in our nation tend to call the word of God, "hate speech." God laws are considered hate speech? Every government has laws. Are those laws considered hate speech as well? Ignorance is prevalent among Americans who say things like that. They have no clue that God is love (I John 4:8). People in our nation are suffering. Mankind has no answers and they still refuse to turn to God. They want to do what is right in their own sight. Yet, what they believe is right is causing even more harm. The Bible clearly says, "*Woe* [sorrow, doom] *unto them that are wise in their own eyes, and prudent in their own sight* (Isaiah 5:21)*!*" When we begin to trust in our own efforts, or in the wisdom and power of human beings alone, then we are destined to be cursed.

On the other hand, when we put our trust in God, then we will be Blessed. Why? Because the Bible says so. "*Blessed [is] the man that trusteth in the LORD, and whose hope the LORD is* (Jeremiah 17:7)." Take the Blessing of Abraham. The Bible says, "*And it shall come to pass, if thou shalt hearken diligently unto the voice of the LORD thy God, to observe [and] to do all his commandments which I command thee this day, that the LORD thy God will set thee on high above all nations of the earth: And all these blessings shall come on thee, and overtake thee, if thou shalt hearken unto the voice of the LORD thy God* (Deuteronomy 28:1-2)." This passage is very straight forward. It says that if we diligently hear and obey the voice of God, that *"all"* these blessings will come and *"overtake"* us. What Blessings? The next several verses describe those blessings in detail. "*Blessed [shalt] thou [be] in the city, and blessed [shalt] thou [be] in the field. Blessed [shall be] the fruit of thy body, and the fruit of thy ground, and the fruit of thy cattle, the increase of thy kine, and the flocks of thy sheep. Blessed [shall be] thy basket and thy store. Blessed [shalt] thou [be] when thou comest in, and blessed [shalt] thou [be] when thou goest out* (Deuteronomy 28:3-6)." Blessed means *empowered to prosper*. Anyone who fights the notion of prosperity is someone who does not know the heart and mind of God. They may as well reject the Blessing and remain in the curse. God wants everything we have, all we do, to be Blessed [prospered]. And there is more.

The next verses declare what the Lord will do for those who will *"diligently hearken"* to the voice of the Lord. "*The LORD shall cause thine enemies that rise up against thee to be smitten before thy face: they shall come out against thee one way, and flee before thee seven ways. The LORD shall command the blessing upon thee in thy storehouses, and in all that thou settest thine hand* unto; and he shall bless thee in the land which the LORD thy God giveth thee. <u>The LORD shall</u> establish thee an holy people unto himself, as he hath sworn unto thee, if thou shalt keep the commandments of the LORD thy God, and walk in his ways. And all people of the earth shall see that thou art called by the name of the LORD; and they shall be afraid of thee. <u>And the LORD shall</u> make thee plenteous in goods, in the fruit of thy body, and in the fruit of thy cattle, and in the fruit of thy ground, in the land which the LORD sware unto thy fathers to give thee. <u>The LORD shall</u> open unto thee his good treasure, the heaven to give the rain unto thy land in his season, and to bless all the work of thine hand: and thou shalt lend unto many nations, and thou shalt not borrow. And <u>the LORD shall</u> make thee the head, and not the tail; and thou shalt be above only, and thou shalt not be beneath; if that thou hearken unto the commandments of the LORD thy God, which I command thee this day, to observe and to do [them]: And thou shalt not go aside from any of the words which I command thee this day, [to] the right hand, or [to] the left, to go after other gods to serve them (Deuteronomy 28:7-14)."

If we diligently hear and obey the Lord, not only will we be Blessed in all that we have, all that we do, but God makes some very specific promises about what He will do. God promises to *"smite"* our enemies that rise up against us. He will *"command the Blessing"* upon our storehouses (bank accounts) and all we set our hands to do. When God commands something, it becomes a law. It's amazing that God would make a law to enforce the Blessing upon any portion of our lives. The Lord promises to *"establish* [raise]" us as a *"holy people"* unto Himself. He will *"make* [appoint, assign, bestow upon]" us plenteous [abundant, excess] in goods, in fruit of the body, fruit of our livestock and fruit of our ground. We serve a God of abundance. When He Blesses us, He does so abundantly. Praise God! No shortages are allowed when you diligently hearken to the voice of God. In Jesus' Name!

It gets even better. The Lord promises to *"open"* to us *"His good treasure."* Stop! Notice that God has *"good treasure"* that He wants to pour out upon us. What does that look like? To start with, it is rain for the land in its season and to Bless the work of our hands. If we are sowing seeds in the ground. We need rain to make it grow. Since we serve the God of abundance, He will make it rain abundantly upon our land. This also has spiritual ramifications. The spiritual rain of God's Spirit will abundantly fall upon us and everything we set our hands to do. Then the scripture describes our abundant position in the earth. We shall *"lend unto many nations"* and *"not borrow."* Let that sink in for a moment. While so many Christians are worrying about paying inflated prices and shortages, God wants to supply us abundantly from *"His good treasure."* I don't know about you, but I receive that for myself in Jesus' Name! Finally, the Lord promises to *"make* [appoint, assign, bestow upon]*"* us, the status of becoming *"the head* [prominent in dignity, power and influence], *and not the "tail."* We shall be *"above only"* and *"not beneath."* These are the promises God will fulfill for all who will *"hearken diligently"* to His commandments, which is the cause for all these Blessings to go into effect.

We just covered the first fourteen verses of Deuteronomy 28 that tell of the Blessing. The next fifty-three (53) verses in Deuteronomy 28 cover the curses that will come upon those who *"wilt not hearken unto the voice of the Lord."* It is well worth your time to read the curses. For they tell what will come upon those who refuse to obey the voice of the Lord. We are emphasizing that the curse has to have a cause. The Bible spells it out in plain speech. The first several verses (Deuteronomy 28:15-25) are basically a reverse of what we read in the Blessing. Everywhere it reads *"Cursed shall thou be"* instead of *"Blessed shalt thou be."* Then, instead of God smiting your enemies, verse 25 reads, *"The Lord shall cause thee to be smitten before thine enemies."* Are you dealing with sickness, disease or other physical ailments? These are effects of the curse. There are many verses concerning how the Lord will make *"pestilences cleave unto you,"* and *"smite you with consumption and with a fever and with an inflammation."* The Lord will smite you with *"the botch* [boils] *of Egypt and with the emerods . . . whereof thou canst not be healed* (Deuteronomy 28:21-22, 27).*"* In other words, sickness and disease will cling to those who refuse to hear and obey the voice of the Lord.

Are you dealing with insanity, blindness or heart ailments? These are the results of the curse according to Deuteronomy 28:28-29. *"The LORD shall smite thee with madness, and blindness, and astonishment of heart: And thou shalt grope at noonday, as the blind gropeth in darkness, and thou shalt not prosper in thy ways: and thou shalt be only oppressed and spoiled evermore, and no man shall save [thee]."* I am taking some time to mention theses curses because often times we accept these things as normal. We consider dementia (even Alzheimer's), and heart ailments as normal. Sure, they are normal under the curse, but they are not from God. Since they are not from God, we must resist what the devil is attempting to put on us. Months before COVID came on the scene, I saw people getting sick and dying for no apparent reason. I inquired of the Lord what was going on. He said that *"television was making them sick."* People were hearing all those medical advertisements and began taking symptoms upon themselves. Overtime, they actually took on those same sickness and diseases that were advertised. The Bible says that *"So then faith [cometh] by hearing, and hearing by the word of God* (Romans 10:17)." We must be careful about what we hear. Words have creative power. If we are not careful, we can find ourselves receiving and speaking things that God did not intend for our lives. We've heard people say, "I'm catching a cold." Why would anyone want to catch a cold? If you caught it, throw it back at the devil. Those are **"words of reception** [words of faith]**,"** inviting that cold **"to come and stay"** in your body. I don't care what the doctor tells you they found in you. Don't say you have it. That's the doctor's report. Don't agree with it! What does the word of God have to say about it? That's the truth you want. Agree with God. That's the truth you speak. According to the word of God, you *"shall have whatsoever"* you say (Mark 11:23). So, say what you want, not what symptoms and medical reports say they found. Sure symptoms come, the Lord always tells me to **"resist"** and symptoms go away.

It is was shameful how the media played upon the minds of people when COVID hit. People began receiving that virus. Some even confess that they would die with COVID. Why? They spoke words of faith for the virus. That's what we can do to ourselves, but it's not the whole story. In the realm of the spirit, the devil and his minions are always speaking sickness, disease and death upon people. That's what they do. The same way God can use the mouth of a man or woman to Bless us, the devil does the same to bring the curse and death upon people. In the spirit realm, one could hear the voices of people calling forth COVID like it were a vicious dog. They wanted people sick and dying. However, there is more. These same people were clearly oblivious to the law of seedtime and harvest. Their wicked prayers and curses were backfiring upon their own lives, and upon their children and their children's children. It became a vicious cycle of *destroy and be destroyed*. People could not get free because they refused to let others go free. Again, we do unto others as we want others to do for us. The Bible also says that what we do for others, God will make happen for us (Ephesians 6:8). That is why we must Bless and not curse others. We will end up cursing ourselves as well. God wants people set free. That devil is the thief.

He comes only to *"steal, kill and destroy."* Jesus came to give us life and that more abundantly (John 10:10), but we have to fight for the right to receive that life. It does not come automatically. It does not come without a fight of faith against the works of the devil. Fight we must, if we want life and not death. It's not enough to say we want our **"right to life"** in this earth. We must fight the good fight of faith, standing on the word of God and doing all in our power to live healthy and whole lives, even in the midst of evil and chaos. Let me emphasize why we do this. It's not only for our health and wellbeing, but for that of our families, and our entire household. We want to keep the *"plague"* of sickness and disease away from our dwellings (Psalm 91:10), because God wants our families Blessed.

Now, in Deuteronomy 28 there are specific curses associated with marriage and family. *"Thou shalt betroth a wife, and another man shall lie with her . . . Thy sons and thy daughters [shall be] given unto another people, and thine eyes shall look, and fail [with longing] for them all the day long: and [there shall be] no might in thine hand* (Deuteronomy 28:30-32)." Adultery is a curse. Yet Christians fill their lives with entertainment, movies and television programs where cheating spouses are the norm. Adulterous and fornicating parents cause their children to be abused. There are so many lost and missing children. Some have been killed. Others have been taken, or even given and sold to other people because of a parent's sin. Is that in the Bible? Yes, it is. *"Thou shalt beget sons and daughters, but thou shalt not enjoy them; for they shall go into captivity* (Deuteronomy 28:41)." This too is a curse. So many children are being abused, by their parents and by other people. Whether by divorce decree, adoption or trafficking, children are being given to others to be afflicted. The world accepts this as normal, the word of God says it's a curse.

The Bible also explains in more detail why curses come upon us (Deuteronomy 28:45-47). *"Moreover all these curses shall come upon thee, and shall pursue thee, and overtake thee, till thou be destroyed; because thou hearkenedst not unto the voice of the LORD thy God, to keep his commandments and his statutes which he commanded thee: And they shall be upon thee for a sign and for a wonder, and upon thy seed for ever. Because thou servedst not the LORD thy God with joyfulness, and with gladness of heart, for the abundance of all [things]."* The last part of that passage really struck me hard when I first read it. The curse can come because we did not serve the Lord with *"joyfulness, and gladness of heart, for the abundance of all things."*

Hearkened to the voice is not enough. We can still be cursed for not being grateful to God. Wow! That carries a powerful punch. So, it's not enough to be obedient. We must be willing, and joyful with a glad heart. Not to do so, is cause for the curse. *"If ye be willing and obedient, ye shall eat the good of the land: But if ye refuse and rebel, ye shall be devoured with the sword: for the mouth of the LORD hath spoken [it]* (Isaiah 1:19-20)."

God exhorted, and I stress, He exhorted me strongly to write this book. This was not something that I chose to do. This was a difficult project to complete, mainly because of the warfare, and the many roadblocks that hindered my progress. Deliverance came at me from various directions while writing this book. I had not expected such drama. In all, I understand now, more than ever, the desire of the Father to set His people free. In fact, God wants all people freed from the curses and traps of the enemy. He doesn't want that devil to cut short our destinies and rob us of the fullness of God's Blessing upon our lives. We are too quick to settle for less than God's best, holding on to things that God wants us to let go of. We also tend to be ignorant of God's love and His desire to give us the best life ever. We think we know, but really we don't know unless the Lord reveals it to us by His Spirit. There are some Christians who continue to confess "what God has Blessed cannot be cursed." Sure, that scripture is true, but not in most of their lives. They've learned how to speak words that sound good, with little proof that the word has worked in their lives.

It's time we all come into the knowledge of the truth. What the Bible says is true. As believers in Jesus Christ, we are ordained for the Blessing. If we choose to go our own way, then the Blessing will become **"*dormant*"** in our lives. It won't work for us, certainly not in the fullness that God intended. If our lives don't line up with the word of God, it's time to inquire of the Lord. Find out what is missing. Find out how to make things right with God. Don't be quick to accept sickness and lack like those who don't know God. You are in the world, but not of the world. You are a citizen of God's Kingdom, where there is no sickness, no death, no lack or any such issue. You are a chosen vessel of God's power and glory, called to preach the gospel, and demonstrate the wonders of our God to heal the sick, raise the dead and cast out devils (Mark 16:17). Why seek the world for answers that are only in God's power? **"*The world needs power not platitude.*"** *"And my speech and my preaching [was] not with enticing words of man's wisdom, but in demonstration of the Spirit and of power: That your faith should not* *stand in the wisdom of men, but in the power of God."* As for Christians in America, we arrogantly think more highly of ourselves than we ought. We have more allegiance to a president or a political party than we do to Jesus Christ Whom we call Lord and Savior. Therefore, the curse lingers upon our land. We don't believe God any more. We want a king to rule over us. Deuteronomy 28:36-37 deals with that situation as well. *"The LORD shall bring thee, and thy king which thou shalt set over thee, unto a nation which neither thou nor thy fathers have known; and there shalt thou serve other gods, wood and stone. And thou shalt become an astonishment, a proverb, and a byword, among all nations whither the LORD shall lead thee."*

What does God have to say about our lives? That is where every believer should ask <u>in every</u> troubling situation. Most often people only approach God when all else has failed. God's word and prayer are the last resort. Many of us don't even realize that we are cursed. Even worse, we are deceived into believing that being "blessed" according to the world's standard is to be esteemed higher than being Blessed of the Lord. Others see no difference in the world's "blessing." They don't care to know the difference either. In these last days, God will reveal the truth about the so called "blessing" that the world offers. It will be proven to be a **"shallow counterfeit."** It's amazing that God gave me the word **"shallow"** to describe the counterfeit blessing of this world. It's **"shallow"** because that so called blessing is really the love of money. It's **"counterfeit"** because it's not the real thing. It's fraudulent. What we called "blessed" in America is nothing but **"covetousness laced with many sorrows."** However, people continue to sell their souls to the devil for money. They will plot and kill for it. As the Bible says, *"For the love of money is the root of all evil: which while some coveted after, they have erred from the faith, and pierced themselves through with many sorrows* (I Timothy 6:10)."

This book is for those who want to be Blessed by the Lord's standards where there is no sorrow added (Proverbs 10:22). It's not about money. The Blessing of the Lord is about the total wellbeing of a person, their family and the communities that they serve. It's about being a Blessing to Bless others. This is the fullness of what God desires for His people. That is why He positioned us in this world, not as the tail, but as the head; above only and never beneath; *"high above all the nations of the earth* (Deuteronomy 28:1)*!"*

God's Purpose For Humanity

Now that we have a handle on what distinguishes the curse from the Blessing, let's briefly discuss why God created human beings in the first place. Over the years, I have met many people who've had a fatalist view of life. They thought that the only purpose for us being alive was so that we could live a miserable life and then die. I also knew a person who believed that if we would ever become "happy" in this life, then God would kill us before we could ever enjoy it. Remember the saying, "life is hell, and then you die?" I have yet to find out where that came from. In any case, none of these thoughts and sayings came from God, the Creator.

In fact, the Bible records God's response to His handiworks at creation. *"And God saw every thing that he had made, and, behold, it was very good* (Genesis 1:31)." Okay, so that was before Adam sinned. Things look a bit different in our world. Yet, God's thoughts and plans towards us have never changed. He wants to do us good all the days of our lives. All things may not be good in the world, but God can take them and use them for our good. As the Bible says, *"And we know that all things work together for good to them that love God, to them who are the called according to [his] purpose* (Romans 8:28)." Even if the devil decides to make us a target of his hostility, God can take what the enemy meant for evil and turn it for our good (Genesis 50:20). I'll share something the Holy Spirit gave me, that most people don't know. Even though the Bible tells us that God is good, not many people believe it. Still, I heard these words in my spirit, **"Always strive to see the good. God is continually good. He has only good. He only desires good for our lives."** Notice how we must **"*strive*"** to see the good. That means it's not obvious. The good is often overshadowed by the evil.

Most people can relate to, and converse about the evil because it's everywhere on the news channels. It would seem that bad things are happening to good people, everyday, all day long. If you believe the report of the media. Personally, I believe the report of the Lord. God is good and there is good happening in this world. We just need to **"*strive*"** to see it. So, we are going to talk about God's good plan for mankind. What was God's purpose for creating us? Why did He send Jesus to restore us back to Himself? Even the angels asked, *"What is man, that thou art mindful of him? And the son* *of man, that thou visitest him? For thou hast made him a little lower than the angels, and hast crowned him with glory and honour. Thou madest him to have dominion over the works of thy hands; thou hast put all [things] under his feet (Psalm 8:4-6)."* Never before was their a creature called "mankind." The angels were curious why God created such a being in His own image and likeness. God clothed mankind in glory and honor and gave us dominion. What was the purpose of all of this? I use to think that God had a sense of humor by choosing to perform His will through weak, flawed human beings. Obviously, God knows something about us that we don't know about ourselves. He created us and knows the potential that lies within each of us. I am grateful to have had an opportunity to visit the Father in Heaven on many occasions. On my very first visit to Heaven, the one question that I wanted answered was, "Why do you love us?" I heard His answer, but I also have to admit that I did not understand the answer God gave me. He said, **"I love my creation because they were created in love."** My response was rather stupid. I said, "Ok," and went on to the next question. I felt really stupid. Here was this huge surge of love going back and forth from the Father, and all I could say was "Ok?" My head could not conceive the love of God. My spirit was receiving it. I knew what the Bible said, but God's love has to be experienced. The best I can share is that God loves us because He is Love. All He can think or do for us is out of His love, and that includes the reason human beings were created.

A friend of mine once said, that the Holy Spirit explained why we should love one another. **"It's the one thing the enemy has no defense against. He cannot comprehend it. So he cannot fight against it." "Love conquers all."** I never thought about it that way. In order for your enemy to launch a successful attack against you, he must be able to track your movements and understand how you think. Think about love. How does a person act when they are attempting to hurt you, and all you do is love them back? They may continue striking at you for a while, but eventually, if you keep loving them, they will walk away and think you're crazy. Why? Love makes no sense to the human brain. Think about what it does to the devil. If we don't react the way he desires, how can he defeat us? We're still talking about why God created us; His purpose for human beings. It's all about love. God created us out of His love for a family. The Father who is Blessed forever (Romans 9:5), created us to be Blessed along side Him for all eternity. Some of you might ask, "Why would a good God place a curse in the earth if His desire was to Bless us?" Good question. Think back to what we said about the law of seedtime and harvest. It is one of the laws that God instituted in the earth. These laws establish *"law and order"* on the planet. Man did not establish these laws. God did. Therefore man cannot change them. He can only live within the constraints of these laws, or choose not to live at all. God placed before us life, death, Blessing or the curse, but it is up to us to choose. These laws are firmly established, but the choice of what to do with them is up to us. We just mentioned seedtime and harvest, but now let's explore the seed.

The purpose of a seed is to bring forth a harvest in the earth. If you have ever placed a seed in dirt, you don't have to direct the seed to grow. *"The seed knows what to do."* Seedtime and harvest is firmly established in the earth. The seed knows that its purpose is to bring forth fruit of its kind. Corn seeds will bring forth corn. It will not bring forth cabbage. Why not? God created every living thing to reproduce after its own kind, *"whose seed is in itself* (Genesis 1:11)." Therefore the plants and trees have seeds within themselves to produce more plants and trees like themselves. Consider mankind. Human beings also have seeds within themselves to produce more of their own kind, however we were not created like other living creatures. From the waters, God called forth fish and fowl. *"And God said, Let the waters bring forth abundantly the moving creature that hath life, and fowl [that] may fly above the earth in the open firmament of heaven* (Genesis 1:20)." From the earth God called forth all the living creatures. *"And God said, Let the earth bring forth the living creature after his kind, cattle, and creeping thing, and beast of the earth after his kind: and it was so* (Genesis 1:24)." Both the waters and the earth were portals (matrices) from which God created life. Mankind was the highest form of life that God created. Out of Himself, God brought forth mankind. Therefore, mankind came forth from the *matrix* of Almighty God. *"And God said, Let us make man in our image, after our likeness: and let them have dominion over the fish of the sea, and over the fowl of the air, and over the cattle, and over all the earth, and over every creeping thing that creepeth upon the earth* (Genesis 1:26)."

Although the Bible says that God made man from the dust of the ground, we did not come from the earth, we came from God. Mankind was created in *the image and likeness* of God (Genesis 1:26). God breathed His breath into his nostrils *"the breath of life; and man became a living soul* (Genesis 2:7)." We are *establishing the origin of the seed called mankind.* Man was created from dust, but he did not come to life until the breath of God entered into that clay mold. It was only then that the life (DNA) of God made mankind a living, speaking spirit like His Father. This was the origin of **"the seed of the Father,"** created to bring forth a specific harvest that God desired in the earth. This was how God created Adam, who was in every way just like God. Ever hear someone say, "the fruit doesn't fall far from the tree?" It means that a child has characteristics similar to that of the parent. This was true of Adam, God's first son born into the earth. That is why God Blessed them saying, *"Be fruitful, and multiply, and replenish the earth, and subdue it: and have dominion* (Genesis 1:28)." God desired to have sons and daughters who would do as their Father did in the earth.

Mankind was originally created as **"the seed of the Father."** So, we said **"the seed knows what to do."** In other words, **"the seed knows what to produce."** How does it know? Where does the seed gets its knowledge? It comes from the Creator. Consider what the Bible says about Adam. *"And out of the ground the LORD God formed every beast of the field, and every fowl of the air; and brought [them] unto Adam to see what he would call them: and whatsoever Adam called every living creature, that [was] the name thereof. And Adam gave names to all cattle, and to the fowl of the air, and to every beast of the field* (Genesis 2:19-20)." How did Adam know what to call those creatures? Apparently God didn't give the man those names. However the knowledge of those names had to come from a source outside of Adam. Yet, the man was created alone. There were no other humans with whom he could have consulted. These were animals that had never existed before, yet Adam, **"the seed of the Father"** knew what to call the animals. Adam knew what to do. How was that possible? God taught the man through **"discernment."** Think about it. Adam was created and **"molded"** to be like God. He was also created to **"resemble"** God in every way. In addition, the DNA [Spirit] of the Father was within him.

Did you ever consider how DNA works in the human body? I'm no scientist, but I do have a basic, yet simple understanding of DNA. The genetic codes are recorded on the DNA strand. That information has to be transcribed and translated in order to produce what the code requires. A similar process happens within the spirit of a man. God's DNA records the necessary information to produce a "god-man" in the individual who has received the Spirit of God through salvation. This is the kingdom within us (Luke 19:10). It is God's glory resident inside the spirit every believer *"which is Christ in you, the hope of glory* (Colossians 1:27)." God's DNA information is transcribed by the Holy Spirit and translated to our human spirit. *"But as it is written, Eye hath not seen, nor ear heard, neither have entered into the heart of man, the things which God hath prepared for them that love him. But God hath revealed [them] unto us by his Spirit: for the Spirit searcheth all things, yea, the deep things of God* (I Corinthians 2:9-10)." Here is how the Lord explained it to me many years ago. **"The script for our lives is revealed to our hearts by the spirit; in the form of a vision; a dream; a spoken word or a 'knowing.' The vision or dream from God is activated by our faith. Our tongue is the ready writer that brings it to pass; just like it was when God spoke and brought all of creation to pass."**[1]

God originally created mankind to look like Him, to sound like Him and to do what He (God) would do in the earth. Does this sound familiar? It should. This is how Jesus lived. He and the Father were one (John 17:21). Jesus only did and said what the Father told Him to say and do (John 5:19). He was the true **"seed of the Father."** And, Jesus produced only what the Father desired in this earth. He set the pattern for all who would be redeemed back to the Father's original design. Jesus is called, *"the last Adam* (I Corinthians 15:45)." He was patterned after the *"first Adam"* to whom God also gave dominion over the earth. God never forced His ways upon the man. He intentionally gave us the freedom to choose whether or not to obey Him. The same was true for Jesus. The Bible says that He was *"in all points tempted"* like we are, but without sin (Hebrews 4:15). Jesus could have chosen to sin. Yet, He understood that sin would have caused Him to violate the covenant He made with the Father. Jesus had to be without sin in order to redeem mankind back to God. Jesus also understood that Adam's sin had changed the DNA of mankind. The **"seed of the Father,"** became **"corrupted,"** [separated and alienated] from its Source DNA. The Spirit and glory of the Father departed from the man. Man was left to survive by his own wits. The Blessing left him, and the curse was activated in the earth. Mankind continued to *"be fruitful and multiply,"* yet, unable to replenish or subdue that which was destroying the earth. The creature [serpent] which mankind was to dominate, began to dominate the man. This was never God's purpose for our lives, yet it was Adam's choice that led humanity into bondage to the curse. God's DNA [His Glory] could not occupy the souls of sinful men. Therefore, it left the earth. But, God's plan for humanity never changed. So He sent Jesus to restore His spiritual DNA

---

1 Matthews, Paula. "Releasing The Glory From Within." *The Glory Of God Revealed Through The Lives Of Ordinary Men.* Atlanta: Spirit & Life Publications[SM], 2014. 43. Print.

back to humanity. God loved us so much that He sent Jesus to restore a **"righteous seed of the Father"** in us. Salvation does not make us perfect. It means that we've made a way for **"God's perfection to be bestowed upon us"** through the person of Jesus Christ. Mind you, the curse is still in the earth. However, God made a way of escape for all who would come to Him. This is how much God loves us. *"For I know the thoughts that I think toward you, saith the LORD, thoughts of peace, and not of evil, to give you an expected end* (Jeremiah 29:11)." God has good planned for every person on the planet, but one must come to Him to find out the *"expected end."* That's exactly what I did. The Bible says, that if any man lacks wisdom to ask God (James 1:5). So I asked.

I wanted to know God's plan not just for me, but for all of humanity. The Lord responded by having me sit down and open my Bible. He took me from Genesis to Revelation. The Lord said, that throughout the Bible, He was **"looking for a family in whom to give an inheritance."** Mankind was created because He [God] desired to have a family in which He could give an earthly inheritance.[2] I expected God to give some grandiose reason for creating mankind. Yet it simple. God wanted a family of His own in this earth. The Father had (and still has) an inheritance that He wants to give us. Things began to make sense. The devil attacks the family that God instituted, because it's all about our inheritance. The devil's attempt to change gender and roles is also about the inheritance God has for us. That devil knows that in order to receive any inheritance one must have proof of his or her identity. The devil has people confused as to whether they are male or a female. Others have been told that one race should be exalted above all other races because of the discrimination from the past. These are **"distractions"** sent to get us out of position to receive what God has for us.

In Christ, all beings are treated the same. *"For as many of you as have been baptized into Christ have put on Christ. There is neither Jew nor Greek, there is neither bond nor free, there is neither male nor female: for ye are all one in Christ Jesus. And if ye [be] Christ's, then are ye Abraham's seed, and heirs according to the promise* (Galatians 3:27-29)." The only identity required for your inheritance is that you are a born again child of God. *"The Spirit itself beareth witness with our spirit, that we are the children of God: And if children, then heirs; heirs of God, and joint-heirs with Christ* (Romans 8:16-17)." One also cannot receive from God without faith. *"But without faith [it is]*

---

2   Matthews, Paula. "Blossoming Into Sonship." *Taught By God*. Atlanta: Spirit & Life Publications[SM], 2022. 142. Print.

impossible to please [him]: for he that cometh to God must believe that he is, and [that] he is a rewarder of them that diligently seek him (Hebrews 11:6)." When we diligently go after God, He will respond to us in earnest. The devil knows this. That is why he sends distractions. Remember that we must **"strive to see the good,"** but when we finally see it, we must *"fight"* the fight of faith to receive it. As the Bible says, the just shall live by faith (Hebrews 10:38). The devil gets people hung up on what we see in the world, but God is always working behind the scenes. That is why the Bible says *"For we walk by faith, not by sight* (II Corinthians 5:7)." Of course we do.

Our fight of faith is against an **"invisible enemy."** The battle begins within, because the Kingdom is within us. That is why the Lord commanded me to **"break family curses."** Some of the distractions placed before us are connected to evil covenants and curses on our family bloodline. Jesus expects us to take up where He left off in destroying the works of the devil (I John 3:8). You cannot destroy what you cannot see. Nor can you, without instructions from the Holy Ghost. We may see something with our eyes, and still not know the truth about what we are seeing. Even as I write this book, there is so much deception in the church, and in the political arena. There are many Christians who are caught up in the madness. Deception is the devil's plan. If I could put a spin on what the Holy Ghost said earlier, I would say it this way, **"Always strive to see the TRUTH. God's word is the Truth. Jesus is TRUTH. He only desires TRUTH for our lives."**

People tend to believe that truth is based upon what they see, feel or know in their senses. Not so! There are things going on in our world in which the media is saying one thing, while the opposite is the truth. You can not explain this to carnal people. They are not interested in hearing what God says is true. That is unfortunate, because the Lord is telling us what is about to happen to such **"and it shall be devastating,"** says God. That is why we must trust God. His word is true. God's word **"exempts** [sanctifies]" us from destruction that comes upon the world. Jesus prayed to the Father, *"Sanctify them through thy truth: thy word is truth* (John 17:17)." Okay, now you know. God's word is truth. Still, few people desire to know the truth. They would rather believe a lie, especially about God. As long as people continue believing a lie, they will never see the goodness of God. To receive what God has, you have to be in pursuit of the truth that is hidden in Christ. *"[It is] the glory of God to conceal a thing: but the honour of kings [is] to search out a matter* (Proverbs 25:2)."

In the world, people are searching for truth *"in all the wrong places."* Our entertainment is a witness against us. Consider how many film and television shows demonstrate the occult, witchcraft and spiritual phenomenon. When human beings go after that which is supernatural, it is because they are searching for a part of themselves that is shrouded in mystery. The Church of Jesus Christ is suppose to teach such things to the world (Ephesians 3:9). Unfortunately, they have not been very good stewards of the mysteries of God (I Corinthians 4:1). The world is reaching for answers about the supernatural and the occult, truths that can only be found in Christ. Remember that God is taking mankind back to His original purpose for all of humanity. That is why Jesus gave His Body the commission to *"Go ye therefore, and teach all nations, baptizing them in the name of the Father, and of the Son, and of the Holy Ghost: Teaching them to observe all things whatsoever I have commanded you: and, lo, I am with you alway, [even] unto the end of the world* (Matthew 28:19-20)." Jesus commanded the Church, the Body of Christ, the People of God, to teach the world Kingdom mysteries.

That was Matthew's gospel account. Mark's gospel comes with a warning. *"And he said unto them, Go ye into all the world, and preach the gospel to every creature. He that believeth and is baptized shall be saved; but he that believeth not shall be damned* (Mark 16:15-16)." The gospel is more than salvation. It is the message about how the power of God's Kingdom supersedes all other kingdom powers in this earth. Jesus didn't just teach a sweet message and go home. No! He taught the word. Afterwards, He demonstrated the power of God's Kingdom to heal the sick, open blind eyes, to make the maimed whole, and the dead to be raised to life again. That's the message people need to hear in our day. Unfortunately, the Church has been silent about the things concerning the Kingdom. Health and healing is God's purpose for humanity. Yet, when the world was hit was COVID, that was the time for the Body of Christ to demonstrate the power of God's Kingdom. Where was the Church? Most were silent, fearful of retaliation from the government. Many closed their doors, never to open again. The people of God were left without hope. Many gave up and died. That was not God's plan. It was their choice to believe the "science" and the experts rather than to believe God. All one needed to ask was, "What would Jesus have done in that situation?" The answer to that question is exactly what the Church should have done, but they did nothing. Thank God for those who chose to obey the Holy Spirit. They receive testimonies of miracles and healings. This is the role of the Church in society. This is how we spread the news of the gospel, with demonstration of God's power against sickness and disease. Plus, there are added benefits to serving God in obedience; a *"spiritual vaccine"* against every disease in this world. This one works without fail. If we hear God's voice and obey Him, He promises *"I will put none of these diseases upon thee* (Exodus 15:26)." What diseases? *"None of the evil diseases of Egypt* (Deuteronomy 7:15)." Egypt represents the world that does not serve God and His purpose. When we obey God, He *"makes a difference"* between His people and those of the world (Exodus 8:23). One of the many benefits of serving God, is that He *"healeth all thy diseases . . . redeemeth thy life from destruction* (Psalm 103:3-4)." He is Jehovah Rapha. *"For I am the Lord that healeth thee* (Exodus 15:26)." God is the Healer but the world does not know it, because many in the Church do not believe. Jesus commanded His followers to go and teach all nations. How can they teach what they have not believed? How can they believe something they have never really heard? How could they have heard if they have never been taught by the Spirit? Going to church and reading the Bible are wonderful things, but if you don't engage the Spirit of the Lord, it profits you very little. One can have *head knowledge* of God without ever experiencing His redemptive power.

The gospel of God's Kingdom has to be experienced. God wants to be known again in the earth. He wants to Bless us. God pronounced the Blessing upon Adam, and Noah, then upon Abraham, and so on. God has a Blessing He wants to deliver. Righteousness, or right standing with God, is also a qualification for the inheritance. In fact, it's part of the spiritual armor that protects us from the schemes of the evil one in this world. *"Wherefore take unto you the whole armour of God, that ye may be able to withstand in the evil day, and having done all, to stand. Stand therefore, having your loins girt about with truth, and having on the breastplate of righteousness* (Ephesians 6:13-14)." Pursue truth and righteousness! They will be your protection in this world of darkness. Mankind was originally created for this. We were born again for this. God wants us to dominate the earth with His Blessing. With such we will commune with Him to create the things that the Father desires in the earth. Think this not strange. We were born again, as the *"resurrected seed of the Father"* to produce *"signs and wonders* (Isaiah 8:18)" in the earth. Mankind could not be born again until Jesus resurrected from the grave. The same resurrection power that raised Jesus from the dead, resides within every believer. *"But if the*

Spirit of him that raised up Jesus from the dead dwell in you, he that raised up Christ from the dead shall also quicken your mortal bodies by his Spirit that dwelleth in you (Romans 8:11)." It is the power of the Holy Ghost that *"quickens"* our spirits and makes us *"alive"* to the Father's will. In this way we have been set apart from the world and made holy [sanctified] for the Father's use. As the **"resurrected seed of the Father"** we can become imitators of God like devoted children (Ephesians 5:1). The same Holy Spirit, the *"breath of life"* that made the first man a *"living soul"* made the born again man a *"quickening spirit* (I Corinthians 15:45)." Therefore, the born again person becomes a living, speaking spirit, like God.

Let me explain what that means. God is a Spirit (John 4:24). He is devoid of what we know as a physical body. Yet, God possesses all power in heaven and in the earth. He has knowledge of all things because God is the Creator of all things. It was the *"breath of the Almighty"* that gave us life (Job 33:4). So, being born again simply reunites us with our Heavenly Father, whether or not you knew Him before. The born again spirit gives us witness that He is our Father and we are His child (Romans 8:16). Science would have you believe that humans descended from apes rather than being created by God. However, truth can be obtained by the born again spirit that has reconciled to God. Would scientist actively pursue God for answers? Not likely. It is the role of believers to answers such questions. We are to *"preach the unsearchable riches of Christ* (Ephesians 3:8)." Our assignment as believers is to *"make all men see what is the fellowship of the mystery"* of Christ (Ephesians 3:9).

That word *Christ* is not Jesus' last name. It is His title; Jesus the Christ, "the Anointed One from God, the Messiah."[3] The word Christ also means "the anointing (supernatural power)" that rests on Jesus and upon every believer. In fact, the name *Christian* means, "little anointed one, or follower of Jesus." Which indicates that our assignment as believers is to emulate Jesus. This statement upsets religious Christians because they don't believe that anyone can do what Jesus did. Yet, the Bible tells us differently. *"Because as He is, so are we in this world* (I John 4:17)." Salvation is not about going to Heaven. It's about bringing Heaven upon the earth. That is why Jesus told us to pray, *"Thy kingdom come. Thy will be done in earth, as [it is] in heaven* (Matthew 6:10)." God desires that we experience days of Heaven upon the earth (Deuteronomy 11:21).

---

3   G5547 - christos - Strong's Greek Lexicon (kjv). Retrieved from https://www.blueletterbible.org/lexicon/g5547/kjv/tr/0-1/

God created this earth for His kids. *"The heaven, [even] the heavens, [are] the LORD'S: but the earth hath he given to the children of men* (Psalm 115:16)." That is why He gave His son Adam dominion in the earth. After Adam, God Blessed Noah and his sons. Later God came to Abraham and told him to leave his country and his father's house, *"unto a land that I will shew thee* (Genesis 12:1)." What God had for Abraham could not be seen with physical eyes. It had to be revealed by the Lord. *"And the LORD said to Abram, after Lot had separated from him: 'Lift your eyes now and look from the place where you are--northward, southward, eastward, and westward; for all the land which you see I give to you and your descendants forever* (Genesis 13:14-15).'" When God released the Children of Israel from slavery in Egypt several hundred years later, it was to go and possess this land which the Lord swore to Abraham to give them. *"When the most High divided to the nations their inheritance, when he separated the sons of Adam, he set the bounds of the people according to the number of the children of Israel* (Deuteronomy 32:8)."

Notice how that verse calls the nations, *"the sons of Adam."* These are the nations according to Abraham's seed, but they can be traced all the way back to the promise God gave Adam. Some people would automatically assume that scripture promise of an inheritance was only for the Jews. I thought so until the Lord explained it to me. It was God's desire for **"a family in whom to give an inheritance."** He didn't mean just one family, the Jews. No! How do we know? Look back at Noah. God gave the Blessing to Noah and his sons for the purpose of repopulating the earth after the flood. At that time, there were no Jews. Humanity was all one family, just like it was in the beginning with Adam and Eve.

Remember, God said that through Abraham, all the families of the earth would be blessed (Genesis 12:3). This promise was for Abraham and his seed but it includes more than the Jews. It includes Christians and everyone who receives Jesus Christ as Lord (Galatians 3:27-29). Notice how believers are addressed as *"one in Christ Jesus."* God, the Father is gathering together the *"whole family in heaven and earth* (Ephesians 3:15)." These are those who have been redeemed by the Blood of Jesus, who have come *"out of every kindred, and tongue, and people, and nation* (Revelation 5:9)." In other words, God has an inheritance to give to everyone who reconciles with Him, regardless of their race, creed or color. After Abraham, the promise of land as an inheritance came first to the Jews, but at creation it was intended for all the people. When Adam left the promise to seek something better on his own, God needed to find another man or a family that would heed His voice. God found Abraham and the inheritance was restored for the Jews first. Why the Jews? It was because of Noah's son Shem. He kept the promise alive while his brothers Japheth and Ham went the way of Adam to do their own thing. This was the first step in restoring God's purpose for humanity. Next, He had to get all the nations back into His Family so that mankind *"are all one"* in His will and purpose.

That is why God had to send Jesus to redeem all men back to God. The curse was still in the earth. Until God found Abraham, it was difficult for mankind to follow the ways of this Invisible God. The Bible highlights the faith of Abraham who was told that he would be the father of many nations even though he was old, and his wife was old and barren. *"And being not weak in faith, he considered not his own body now dead, when he was about an hundred years old, neither yet the deadness of Sara's womb: He staggered not at the promise of God through unbelief; but was strong in faith, giving glory to God; And being fully persuaded that, what he had promised, he was able also to perform. And therefore it was imputed to him for righteousness* (Romans 4:19-22)." Abraham believed God and it was counted to him as righteousness. Therefore he was made *"the heir of the world* (Romans 4:13)."

God told Abraham that his descendants would be enslaved for over four hundred years. During that time the people were estranged from the God of their fathers and forced to serve idols. *"And also that nation, whom they shall serve, will I judge: and afterward shall they come out with great substance* (Genesis 15:14)." I felt led to mention this parallel with those enslaved in Egypt with those of us who have been under the same spirit of pharaoh in our day. God is about to judge the nations who have forced His people to serve idols, and we will come out with *"great substance."* This will be the greatest wealth transfer in history. Abraham's seed plundered the nation of Egypt (Exodus 12:36). The same is about to happen in our day, **"and very soon says," God.** The nations of the earth will have to pay for how they have treated the people of God. The judgment of God does not come to destroy a nation. It comes so that people would repent and serve God. It comes as an answer to Pharaoh who question Moses, whom God sent to deliver the people out of bondage. *"And Pharaoh said, Who [is] the LORD, that I should obey his voice to let Israel go? I know not the LORD, neither will I let Israel go* (Exodus 5:2)." When it was all said and done, Pharaoh learned about the Lord. It cost him his life and that of his soldiers. In the end, God's people were set free. They were saved. Salvation was just the first step. The same is true with us today. God will deliver us from the power of satan, but we have to do what is necessary to stay free. God gave them commandments, but they could not keep them. Still His desire was to give them an inheritance, but they were fearful of the giants in the land. Okay, let's talk.

Look at how many Christians who say they believe God, but yet they are afraid of the giants in the land. There are the giants of poverty, lack, sickness and disease, and don't forget tyrannical leaders of government and business who want to force God's people to turn from Him to serve idols. Too many people are hiding in church buildings and hiding behind the Name of Jesus, but not exhibiting any power to slay the giants in the land. The curse has brought the giants to the forefront of the world stage. They are huffing and puffing as it they can destroy people, but our God is bigger and more powerful. When are we going to demonstrate that fact? The world is waiting for a showdown with Goliath, and God is about to send it, and send it so fast that the giant will fall before he even knew what hit him. We are dealing with evil covenants and curses and breaking their hold so we can enjoy the Blessing of the Lord. Sometimes that means taking down a giant in the face of fearful onlookers. So be it. In Jesus' Name!

Now, let us continue with the seed and God's purpose for humanity. In the beginning, God gave man dominion and the seed. In these last days, God is restoring that dominion by faith in Jesus Christ, who is the word of God (John 1:1,14). Jesus came to deal with the curse so that all men could be free to follow God. It's the only way to escape the curse and the penalty of death. The Bible also tells us that Jesus was the seed of Abraham (Galatians 3:16). Just like Abraham, God appointed Jesus *"heir of all things* (Hebrews 1:2)." The Bible let's us know that those who receive Jesus are *"joint heirs"* with Him (Romans 8:17)." Do you understand what it means to be a *"joint heir?"* It means that what Jesus inherited, we, the Body of Christ, also inherit, singularly and jointly. God's inheritance is not divided. We are joint owners, each and every one of us. God made Jesus *"heir of all things."* Are you ready for this? If you are in Christ, you are also an *"heir of all things."* Some religious people would argue that this is referring to "all spiritual things." Not so! Look at what the Bible says that Jesus received, by coming to earth, dying on the cross and resurrecting again. *"Worthy is the Lamb that was slain to receive power, and riches, and wisdom, and strength, and honour, and glory, and blessing* (Revelation 5:12)." This is what Jesus inherited in the earth. As joint heirs with Him, this is also what we receive when we reconcile our lives back to God through Him. Think about it. Our inheritance as sons and daughters of God includes *"power, and riches, and wisdom and honour, and glory and blessing."* And, this is just the beginning. This was God's plan for all of humanity. It's still His plan for us this day!

When the Lord first revealed this to me years ago, He also said that He had set aside enough wealth in the earth so that **"every person could be a millionaire."** What happened? The devil decided to cheat the masses out of their inheritance and hoard it for himself and his wicked kids. God has set aside an immeasurable amount of wealth and riches, both spiritual and physical. It is available for those who come to Him. These are treasures that are hidden in Christ. *"And I will give thee the treasures of darkness, and hidden riches of secret places, that thou mayest know that I, the LORD, which call [thee] by thy name, [am] the God of Israel (Isaiah 45:3)."*

God has so many wonderful things for His Family. That devil knows it all too well. That's why he fights so hard against those who serve Jesus. He knows about the power and wealth that has been given to us. The devil may have stolen it for a season, but in the end **"what was stolen must be returned."** Those are the exact words, the Lord spoke to me. We have a covenant that makes provision for handling thieves. *"But if he be found, he shall restore sevenfold; he shall give all the substance of his house (Proverbs 6:31)."* Satan has to give up everything in his wicked house, and he will. In these last days, the wealth of the sinner (Proverbs 13:22) is about to come into the hands of those who trust God and who walk by faith. This is God's justice at work. He will recompense His people for what they have suffered. Not only will God recover all, but He will repay us for the damages suffered. This is how God will **"recover the earth"** for His purposes. It's called **"vengeance and recompense."** God will avenge us speedily (Luke 18:8).

The Lord demonstrated this in a *vision. I had been praying and praising when in the realm of the spirit I saw a great dragon hovering in the heavens over a city. The belly of the dragon was large, as if it were so full that is was hanging low. As I continued to pray and praise, I found myself flying in the sky towards that dragon with a sword in my hands. My feet were moving as if I was stepping on a ladder into the heavens. This was no staircase. These were multiple angels lifting me in their hands, getting me closer to that dragon.*

And when I got within striking distance, I took that sword and cut the belly of that dragon from front to tail. Out of his belly came wealth, money, gems, precious metals and all forms of wealth. It was so much that I had the angels gather it all in bags. I told them to make sure that nothing would fall to the ground. We gathered all of the wealth that great dragon, the old serpent, the devil who is called satan, had confiscated from the people of the earth.[4] This is how much God truly loves us. He enlisted the angels to recover stolen goods from the enemy. Yet, I had to see into the world of the invisible. I had to speak what the Lord put in my spirit to release into earth's atmosphere. The angels came in response to my words (Daniel 10:12).

Everything, in this earth is about to be returned to God. The Bible says, "*The earth [is] the LORD'S, and the fulness thereof; the world, and they that dwell therein* (Psalm 24:1)." Jesus came to restore it all back to the Father; the people, the earth and all of its possessions. It all belongs to God, and we are His heirs. Therefore it all belongs to us. God is a good Father who wants to give us an inheritance. Jesus said that there was no one good but God (Matthew 19:17). Think about it. If you were a parent that had immeasurable wealth, wouldn't you give it to the **"rightful heirs"** and not just to anyone? Wouldn't they have to fulfill specific requirements? Wouldn't you give it to them to honor your family name? The Bible says that a *"good man"* would leave an inheritance for his descendants (Proverbs 13:22).

Consider Adam and Eve. God made them heirs of the entire world, yet their **"proving ground"** was the Garden of Eden. They were created for the Blessing. It was their **"rod of righteousness"** to rule the planet. The serpent deceived them into forfeiting their inheritance. The Bible says that Eve was deceived, however Adam was not (I Timothy 2:14). God gave the commandment directly to Adam. He knew that death would be the consequence of his disobedience (Genesis 2:17). However, the serpent told the woman, "*Ye shall not surely die* (Genesis 3:4)." Adam was responsible for making sure his family obeyed God. Yet, they were confronted with words that negated what God commanded, and they believed the serpent. Why? They knew what God said, but with their eyes, they saw something different. It was what Eve *"saw"* that captured her imagination. Her lust enticed her to eat of the forbidden fruit, but she was not alone. The Bible says, "*she took of the fruit thereof, and did eat, and gave also unto her husband with her; and he did eat* (Genesis 3:6)." Evidently, Adam waited to see if some-

---

4 Matthews, Paula. "The Vision Of That Great Dragon." *It's Time To Recover All!*. Atlanta: Spirit & Life Publications℠, 2016. 37. Print.

thing would happen to his wife. Then he ate the fruit after her. This would be his argument against what God said. Notice how the enemy likes to challenge what God said. But, it was the woman's lust that cause her to be deceived. It's one thing to be deceived by another. It's yet another thing to *"deceive"* our own hearts through lust for what is forbidden.

What they desired line up with what they saw. That's the moment they turned away from God. Isn't that just like human nature? We believe what we see, or what we feel or think. That makes us vulnerable to deception because of what <u>we want</u> "to believe is true." In our hearts we may know that something is not true. If our desire is to make it true anyway, then we deceive ourselves. So, when Christians say, "God knows my heart." Sure He does (Jeremiah 17:9). God knows is the one who searches our hearts. This is why we must let God take the reins of our hearts. We get born again to take on a new nature that is of God. Otherwise we, being called to the Blessing, may find ourselves living in the curse. I know something about that. This was my story for many years. I would read the Bible and find all those good things God said He would do for us. Yet none of those things were happening in my life. In my spirit, I knew that I was out of line with God, but everyone around me kept speaking against the Bible. So many were speaking as though what was in that Bible was **"unattainable."**

In my spirit I knew something was missing. I was in a denominational church that did not believe in the Holy Ghost nor in the gifts of the Spirit. It got to the point that I could not even tell them what I was feeling. It's a hard thing to hear someone close to you say, "Who do you think you are? Do you think you are better than us? Why should you deserve to have a better life?" I didn't have answers for them. I just knew in my heart, there was more to God than what I was seeing. I continued going to church, but I withdrew from the people. They seemed to be satisfied with religious tradition. I was not. I wanted more. I wanted the Blessing of the Bible to manifest in my life. My heart's desire for the Blessing has never changed. I matriculated through the world system with some success, but it was not the Blessing I desired. Quickly I learned that there are many so called "blessings" with many strings attached. Still, my heart went after God. Some people saw my anointing and just assume that it is because I "never went through anything in life." That is so far from the truth. The anointing that I carry is because of my **"brokenness"** before God. I am free in His presence. God can say anything to me about me. I am free to do the same before Him. We have a strong Father-daughter relationship. I've been through so many traumatic things, yet God is **"continually healing them all."** I want to be made *"whole."* Like the woman with the issue of blood, I keep saying to myself, *"If I may touch but his clothes, I shall be whole* (Mark 5:28).*"*

In fact, I had an experience years ago. It was a time of intense warfare, and a high praise came upon me. I found myself *in the realm of the spirit,* in the temple the Prophet Isaiah described (Isaiah 6:1). *Then I saw the Lord. The train of His robe filled the temple. He wasn't seated. The Lord was walking. Whether is was towards His throne or away from it, I never knew. But, I began walking behind Him. Then I fell and began crawling behind the Lord trying to touch the hem of His robe. The more I praised, the more I found myself desperately reached for Him in that vision.* That is my heart towards the Lord. I just want to be made whole. I want what Jesus died and resurrected to give me. I also want God's destiny for my life. This is why I obeyed when the Lord told me to **"break family curses."** I not only broke them off of my family, but I prayed the same off of the Church, the nations and all of the families of the earth. It's not so much about getting rid of curses. It's more about **"receiving what God has for us."** It's in the process of receiving the good, that the evil must be released. The same is true of sin. We don't have to strive not to sin. We **"strive to see"** and receive the goodness of God in the land of the living. What we see is what we believe. That is what happened to Adam and Eve. They saw something, not from God, but from their adversary the devil. It's important that we seek those things that are above, where Christ is (Colossians 3:1-2).

The Lord will show us what we need to know, if we would only ask Him. God will show us His good in the midst of what the world would call disastrous condition. This is why we must walk by faith, not by sight. What we see and experience with our senses is subject to change (II Corinthians 4:18). What God tells us does not change. God's purpose for humanity is to give us an inheritance. The devil's plan is to deceive and **"distract"** us so that we forfeit our inheritance. We are entitled to an inheritance because of our relationship with the Father. The Son, Jesus Christ was the sacrifice and redeemer who covenanted with the Father to restore our inheritance. The Holy Ghost is the **"executor"** of God's inheritance. God's riches are deemed, *"unsearchable."* Without the Holy Spirit guiding us, we can't even begin to see or envision the good things God has for us. And yet, there are so many Christians who have been taught not to believe in the Holy Spirit.

Our inheritance is supernatural. It comes from the realm of the spirit, but it can only be revealed by the Holy Spirit. If God's people shun the Holy Ghost because of tradition, they will never see their inheritance this side of Heaven. On the other hand, the devil's kids are willing to steal, kill and destroy for anything they can get. The Lord is putting an end to this robbery. He is reclaiming everything for His glory alone.

Here is the reality of our human existence. Whether we want to admit it or not, Almighty God originally created mankind to be His **"exact clone."** Some religious people would have a fit about my saying this, but stay with me. We want to summarize God's purpose and design for mankind. Why is this important? The curse is a **"disruption, a glitch"** in God's purpose. Until we understand the purpose, we won't know the importance of **"disarming"** the glitch. We also won't be able to understand what God is doing in these last days before Jesus returns. Deception is rampant because the devil, who is mankind's enemy, does not want us to learn the truth about God's purpose for our lives. God wants a family in the earth; one that is created in His own image and likeness, to remain with Him for all eternity. As long as people are deceived, the devil can keep them in the dark about who they really are. Mankind was never created to be a pawn of the evil one, nor to die separated from their Creator. We were created for a specific purpose that cannot be performed apart from God. Sin separated us from God. Sin also brought forth the curse and death. Adam made that choice for all of mankind. Jesus came to restore back to us eternal life. If we continue to sin against God and not repent, then we will continue to reap the curse and death.

God is reaching out to humanity. It's not His desire that anyone is loss. God's truth is all around us. It's the devil who wants to destroy us. Therefore he is diligent to keep us ignorant about our relationship with the Heavenly Father. Yes, I said it. God is <u>our</u> Heavenly Father. He birthed mankind from creation from *"one blood"* to dwell on the earth and determined our appointed times and the boundaries of our habitation. We are *"the offspring of God* (Acts 17:26, 28-29)." We came out of the **"spiritual loins"** of the Creator. The heathen vehemently fights against the notion that God is our Creator. There are Christians who are fighting against the reality that they have been **"recreated"** to be like our Heavenly Father. Both are estranged from the truth about who they really are and why God created them. The late Dr. Myles Munroe said, that *"where purpose is not known abuse is inev-*

itable." He also said, *"If you want to know the purpose of the thing, never ask the thing." "The purpose is only found in the mind of the creator of the thing."*[5] That is what I am attempting to do in this chapter. I didn't consult flesh and blood to learn about God's purpose for mankind. I went directly to God, the Creator. He directed me to the Bible (The Word of God) which reflects both the mind, will and purpose of God.

God created us for His purpose. *"The Lord hath made all things for himself: yea, even the wicked for the day of evil* (Proverbs 16:4)." The Bible says that when God created man, even the angels marveled to see this being that was in every way like God (Psalm 8:4-6). This was Adam, God's first son on earth. He was the perfect clone of His Father, until he departed from trusting in God. Yet the Bible says that Adam lived to be nine hundred and thirty years old (Genesis 5:5). The man did not physically die right after he sinned against God. He had three sons. Adam lived another eight hundred years after his youngest son Seth was born. So, did God lie when He said to Adam, *"for in the day that thou eatest thereof thou shalt surely die* (Genesis 2:17)?" Not at all. The Apostle Paul wrote, *"by one man sin entered into the world, and death by sin: and so death passed upon all men, for that all have sinned* (Romans 5:12)." So what happened? How did this death come to pass if Adam did not physically die right away?

This was death of a relationship between God and His beloved creation, mankind. Adam left the covenant [agreement] of life that he had with God, and chose death, not just for himself, but for all of humanity. God's Spirit was what gave man life. Death for humanity began when the Spirit of God departed from the man and the process of dying began. It reminds me of what Jesus said. *"I am the vine, ye are the branches . . . If a man abide not in me, he is cast forth as a branch, and is withered; and men gather them, and cast them into the fire, and they are burned* (John 15:5-6)." What happens to a branch that is separated from the vine? It dies. That is what happened to man when He separated from God. The man was cut off from his Source of life. Therefore he had no choice but to die. Without the vine, the branch can do nothing but die. Such was the case with man. He did **"surely die"** until Jesus came to restore to us life, and that more abundantly (John 10:10). Now mankind has a choice. We can choose our outcome in this life. There are only two choices; life or death, the Blessing or the curse. The Blessing brings life (Deuteronomy 30:19)."

---

5   Munroe, Myles. "God's Purpose In Creation." *The Purpose And Power of Women*. New Kensington, PA: Whitaker House, 2001. 31. Kindle Ed.

The first thing that manifested after Adam sinned, was the death of their innocence. *"And the eyes of them both were opened, and they knew that they were naked* (Genesis 3:7)." Before their eyes were opened, the Bible says that they were naked and not ashamed (Genesis 2:25). After their eyes were opened they were ashamed. They *"hid themselves from the presence of the Lord God* (Genesis 3:7-8)." Guilt and shame forced them to hide from the same God with whom they had been a companion. What changed? God's love towards them never changed. His purpose for their lives never changed either. So, what was the change? Mankind fell from grace and was reduced to an **"empty shell"** made from the dust of the earth. The *"crown"* of glory and honor left them. They were now in the world, naked, ashamed, and alone. They made clothing from fig leafs to cover themselves (Genesis 3:7). It wasn't good enough to replace the glory of God that had covered them. Sin separated the holy God from sinful men. *"Behold, the Lord's hand is not shortened, that it cannot save; neither his ear heavy, that it cannot hear: But your iniquities have separated between you and your god, and your sins have hid his face from you, that he will not hear (Isaiah 59:1-2)."*

From that day until this, all men have sinned and come short of the glory of God (Romans 3:23). The curse that God pronounced upon Adam, came upon all of creation. *"And unto Adam he said, cursed [is] the ground for thy sake; in sorrow shalt thou eat [of] it all the days of thy life; Thorns also and thistles shall it bring forth to thee; and thou shalt eat the herb of the field; In the sweat of thy face shalt thou eat bread, till thou return unto the ground; for out of it wast thou taken: for dust thou [art], and unto dust shalt thou return* (Genesis 3:14-19)." Everything in creation became cursed because of one man's sin. Whereas mankind was Blessed by God to live forever, after Adam sinned, we were destined to be cursed forever. What was meant to bring life, brought death instead. It seemed like God's plan for an earthly family was doomed. Yet, God had found another man with whom He would make covenant. He found Noah, then Abraham, but the curse still haunted mankind.

Then God found another man willing to sacrifice His life for us all. That man was God's only begotten Son, Jesus Christ who took the curse for our sakes. The Father and the Son made a covenant for the benefit of mankind. *"He shall see of the travail of his soul, [and] shall be satisfied: by his knowledge shall my righteous servant justify many; for he shall bear their iniquities. Therefore will I divide him [a portion] with the great, and he shall divide the spoil with the strong; because he hath poured out his soul unto death: and he was numbered with the transgressors; and he bare the sin of many, and made intercession for the transgressors* (Isaiah 53:11-12)."

Almighty God wants to restore the glory back to mankind. It is the desire of God, that all men would be saved, and come into the knowledge of the truth. What truth? *"For there is one God* (I Timothy 2:4-5)." Is this not the first commandment? *"Thou shalt have no other gods before me . . . Thou shalt not bow down thyself to them, nor serve them: for I the LORD thy God [am] a jealous God, visiting the iniquity of the fathers upon the children unto the third and fourth [generation] of them that hate me; And shewing mercy unto thousands of them that love me, and keep my commandments* (Exodus 20:3-6)." Herein lies the reason for so many generational curses; idolatry [serving other gods]. This sin becomes an iniquity that is in the spiritual bloodline to the third and fourth generations. Yet, God says, **"its time to repent!"** He wants to Bless us.

There is also another truth that God wants mankind to understand. There is only *"one mediator between God and men, the man Christ Jesus* (I Timothy 2:4-6)." Jesus said it Himself, *"I am the way, the truth, and the life: no man cometh unto the Father, but by me* (John 14:6)." One god and one mediator infuriates so many people. They hate this truth and seek other mediums to tell them what they want to hear. Still, **"there is no other way to truth"** except through Jesus Christ. This is God's purpose for humanity. This is the covenant God has ordained to Bless all the families of the earth. So, what happens when we make covenants that are against God's purpose for their lives? We will explore that next.

Covenants And Consequences

In its simplest definition, *a covenant* is an agreement made between two or more people. It can be a formal pact, a treaty or a partnership arrangement between parties. In a covenant each party agrees to carryout certain criteria in order to receive specific benefits from the other. Usually penalties are expressly stately as *"evil consequences"* if either party does not carry out his or her part of the agreement. While doing research for this chapter, the Lord gave me a scriptural description of a covenant. *"That which was lacking on your part, they have supplied* (I Corinthians 16:17)." Apostle Paul talked about a covenant in terms of a ***"partnership"*** arrangement where what one person lacked, another was able to supply. This Bible description lets us know that **"a person enters into covenant because of their perception that someone else can supply what is lacking in their lives."** For example, a person desires a loan and enters into covenant with a bank because that institution has money they need. An exchange is made to fulfill a perceived need (lack) that the other person is expected to supply.

The greatest covenant available to mankind is the one that God made with His Son Jesus Christ. His Blood covenant is for both the redemption, provision and protection of every human being. It's available for everyone, even for those who don't yet follow after God. Jesus sacrificed His life for the entire world (John 3:16). This is God's love towards all of humanity. What differentiates God's covenant from others, is that the parties are *"all in."* Each party brings all they have to the table. God gave His only Son for this covenant. Jesus gave His life for this covenant, and those who receive are also expected to give their all for the sake of this agreement.

In many ways, it's a marriage of personal interests and resources. We saw this in the New Testament church. *"And the multitude of them that believed were of one heart and of one soul: neither said any [of them] that ought of the things which he possessed was his own; but they had all things common* (Acts 4:32)." Believers should have all things in common. Everything God has belongs to us, and everything we have belongs to Him. King David had a revelation of this when He dedicated offerings to the building of the temple. *"But who am I, and what is my people, that we should be able to offer so willingly after this sort? For all things come of thee, and of thine own have we given thee* (I Chronicles 29:14)." This is the heart posture of those who are in covenant with the God who gives to us freely. The Lord is honored when we freely give back to Him what was His from the beginning. God's covenant is the way to transfer the abundance of Heaven into the lives of His people here on earth. In fact, **"covenants are spiritual vehicles"** established by God, to be used to **"facilitate the work of Heaven"** upon the earth. Evil covenants, are **"unauthorized vehicles"** used mostly to thwart the will of God in the earth.

Now, there are some Christians who have entered into evil covenants believing that they were doing the will of God. In some cases, these agreements may be considered the same as witchcraft (I Samuel 15:23). Sometimes it is done in ignorance and God will show mercy. Still, they operating a spiritual vehicle without a license, without permission or proper instruction from the Lord. Not knowing the will of God, nor the **"spiritual rules of the road"** causes many to violate God's covenant. Some will crash. Others will burn if they don't turn back to God's way of doing things. These are some of the **"evil consequences"** of covenanting against Almighty God. It's time to repent and follow the rules that God established in the earth. The Lord understands that some of us have entered into covenants not realizing that there would be negative consequences to pay. What we thought was for our good, ended up working against God's will for our lives. People enter into covenants, even evil covenants, without realizing that there are **"unseen"** consequences associated with every agreement.

These consequences occur because God's people don't understand why God's covenants were instituted in the first place. God covenanted with mankind, as He told Abraham, *"To be a God unto thee, and to thy seed after thee* (Genesis 17:7)." It's a pledge of loyalty to Almighty God and His ways. The same is true of salvation. When we say Jesus is Lord, it is a pledge of loyalty to His will and no longer to our own. That is why covenants made outside of God's will always bring about **"evil consequences."** When we takes what God devised for His will and twist it to fit our own will, we will face **"evil consequences."** God has always referred to those who stray from His covenant as "adulterous." They promised themselves to Almighty God and yet go *"whoring after other gods* (Judges 2:17)." God's covenant was designed to be a **"legally binding agreement for life."** In fact, the very first covenant was made between God and His Son Jesus Christ, before the worlds were formed. It was instituted for the redemption of mankind.

"And all that dwell upon the earth shall worship him, whose names are not written in the book of life of the Lamb slain from the foundation of the world (Revelation 13:8)." This covenant with Jesus set both a **"legal and spiritual precedent"** for all covenants. It established God's **"original intent for the planet."** *"For this [is] good and acceptable in the sight of God our Saviour; Who will have all men to be saved, and to come unto the knowledge of the truth. For [there is] one God, and one mediator between God and men, the man Christ Jesus; Who gave himself a ransom for all, to be testified in due time* (I Timothy 2:3-6)."

God's covenant was instituted for the wellbeing of mankind under the rule and reign of Heaven's government. *"The Lord hath prepared his throne in the heavens; and his kingdom ruleth over all* (Psalm 103:19)." His covenant purpose for mankind has not changed. No matter what agreement we make amongst ourselves, it will not supercede what God has covenanted for the earth. God's covenant is law, whether or not we choose to honor it. *"Know therefore that the LORD thy God, he [is] God, the faithful God, which keepeth covenant and mercy with them that love him and keep his commandments to a thousand generations* (Deuteronomy 7:9)." Haters of God will continue to covenant with death. They will continue to stand on their agreements with hell because they find comfort in their lies and hide themselves under falsehoods. Yet they cannot overturn what God has destined for earth and its people. And, in the day of His judgment, their lies shall not stand. Even now, we witness wicked rulers who believe they can **"overthrow"** the covenant of God, simply because they have banded together against the Lord and His anointed. They believe in the power of agreement, but it does not stand against the Father, the Son and the Holy Ghost. They three all agree and are invincible in power.

God's covenant has **"evil consequences"** for evil doers who conspire against His covenant people. *"Behold, they shall surely gather together, [but] not by me: whosoever shall gather together against thee shall fall for thy sake. Behold, I have created the smith that bloweth the coals in the fire, and that bringeth forth an instrument for his work; and I have created the waster to destroy. No weapon that is formed against thee shall prosper; and every tongue [that] shall rise against thee in judgment thou shalt condemn. This [is] the heritage of the servants of the LORD, and their righteousness [is] of me, saith the LORD* (Isaiah 54:15-17)." Anyone who conspires against God's people will fall. Sure weapons form, but they shall not prosper. We stand on our covenant and decree what God has promised (Job 22:28). The weapons of our warfare are not carnal, but mighty through God to the pulling down of strongholds (II Corinthians 10:4). The devil's weapon of choice is deception beginning with thoughts and imaginings that exalt themselves above what God has said. We saw what happened to Adam and Eve. The serpent questioned, *"Yea hath God said?"* That devil did the same to Jesus.

Matthew's gospel tells what happened when Jesus was baptized, *" . . . and, lo, the heavens were opened unto him, and he saw the Spirit of God descending like a dove, and lighting upon him: And lo a voice from heaven, saying, This is my beloved Son, in whom I am well pleased* (Matthew 3:16-17)." All the earth heard the voice from Heaven. After which the Holy Spirit led Jesus into the wilderness. For what purpose? *" . . . to be tempted of the devil."* Get this. Right after Jesus is baptized, God by His Spirit sends the man into the *"wilderness to be tempted"* by that devil. Why would God do such a thing? There is another **"spiritual precedent"** here. God had spoken by His Spirit. He announced to the world, who Jesus was. Now it was time for Jesus to *fight the good fight of faith*, proving to the devil that He was indeed whom God said He was. How do we know? When that devil first meets Jesus he said to Him, *"If thou be the Son of God . . .* (Matthew 4:1-3)." He doesn't just say it once, but that devil says it again. When that doesn't work, the Bible says, *"Again, the devil taketh him up into an exceeding high mountain, and sheweth him all the kingdoms of the world, and the glory of them; And saith unto him, All these things will I give thee, if thou wilt fall down and worship me."* First of all, how did the devil take Jesus upon on a mountain. This was not a physical act. It was a vision that the devil showed to Jesus.

This was the Son of God. The devil could not move His body, nor touch His spirit. The devil uses the imagination. This is why the Bible tells us to *"cast down every imagination and high things that exalts itself against the knowledge of God."* The devil showed Jesus all the kingdoms of the world and their wealth. He offered it all to the Son of God, if only Jesus would bow down and worship the evil one. That's the covenant arrangement the devil wants from every human being. He wants us to bow down and worship him. Notice how Jesus dealt with the devil in that wilderness. He stood on the covenant saying, *"It is written."* Jesus never spoke how He felt or what He thought. Jesus spoke the word only, and the temptation ended (Matthew 4:8-11). This is an example of why it is important to know our covenant and take a stand against the evil one. The devil knows what the

Bible says. He used it against Jesus. Therefore Jesus had to be led by the Holy Spirit in order to stop the devil in his tracks. We must also do the same. Satan wants the people to worship him, while God continues with His desire to raise a righteous family for an inheritance in this earth. Here is the thing. God gave mankind dominion over the earth. Therefore, **"He can do nothing in the earth without the cooperation of another man (or woman)."** I really hope you are hearing this. So often people want to blame God for the evil that happens in the earth. Truth is, we are in charge, at least in part. It's God's earth. However, when He gave us dominion it was so that we could *"dress and keep"* what God placed in our care (Genesis 2:15). In other words, we are *"stewards"* of God's earth. We will be judged on how well we have stewarded that which was given to us. As the Bible says, it is necessary that stewards *"be found faithful* (I Corinthians 4:2)."

As stewards of this earth, we are also expected to be *"co-creators"* with Almighty God to produce everything this planet and its people require. That is why God Blessed mankind saying, *"Be fruitful and multiply, REPLENISH the earth and SUBDUE it* (Genesis 1:28)." Within that covenant Blessing, mankind was given his assignment for the earth. When Adam broke covenant, God had to find another man, in which to give an inheritance. Let me stop here for a moment. Some of you might be offended that God said He was *"seeking a family"* yet He started looking for a man. There is a reason for this. God made man first. By doing so, He ordered *"the chain of command"* for the family in this earth. This is for the protection of all members of the family. Notice that in the case of Adam and Eve. The woman was deceived by the serpent and ate of the fruit. Then she gave it to her husband and he ate of it. The Bible never credits the woman with sin. No! Since the man was created first, and He was given the command directly from God, the sin was placed upon Adam not his wife.

People don't realized that God has a Kingdom order for the family. As believers, we are a royal family. There are *"rules of royal succession"* in place. It's not about the man being over the woman. It's about the man being first in line to rule under God's Kingdom. When the man is absent or unable to rule, then the woman can rule in his stead. If the parent is not able to rule, then the firstborn child can rule, and so on. This is God's Kingdom order. *"But I would have you know, that the head of every man is Christ; and the head of the woman [is] the man; and the head of Christ [is] God* (I Corinthians 11:3)." The same is true for our divine inheritance. Under the old covenant, it came down the Father's lineage to the firstborn male, then to the next male, and so on. However, in the absence of a father or a male heir, God gave the family inheritance to the daughters (Numbers 27:7). Under the new covenant with Jesus Christ, God treats every son and daughter like the firstborn. We all have an inheritance regardless of our position or rank in God's family. This inheritance is for the fulfillment of God's covenant promise for each of our lives.

God not only covenants with individual believers, but He also arranges for us to covenant with one another in partnerships for various assignments. These covenant arrangements are necessary for restoring the glory of God in the earth. Think about this. If Adam had never sinned, every human being would be in his or her rightful place as heir of God's Kingdom. However, after sin, everyone was out of order because human beings were forced to seek their own way in this world. For the most part, we are very much out of order, even today. We follow the Spirit to one place only to find out that our covenant connections have moved. Things are out of order in that place. As an obedient son or daughter, God may have us remain in that place to straighten things out a bit, while waiting on another covenant connection to take us to the next level. I recall being confused about all the changes in my life. The Lord would tell me I'm on my way back to a certain country, and then He told me to wait in another city because the enemy set a trap for me. Then while in that city, He told me to go to another in response to a spiritual distress call. I get to that city and He commands me to buy property in yet another city several hundred miles away. All the while the enemy is following me with threatenings. What's up with that?

To spiritual onlookers, it seemed like a spiritual game of cat and mouse. To religious folk, it seemed like I was confused, and not hearing God correctly. Then one day, the Holy Spirit made me laugh out loud. He gave me a *vision of my going from place to place with the enemy following after me. In the vision I was chasing God and the enemy was chasing me, but it wasn't really me. It was the enemy chasing God. When God sends us somewhere, we go as His agent. Therefore in the realm of the spirit, it's not me, it's God going from place to place. Unbeknownst to that devil, his people were chasing after God . . . and many found Him along the way.* Many of those who chased after me for evil, were thrown off their high horses like Saul and converted. What they meant for evil, God turn for their good and made them believers. So, why the chase? In my observation, the enemy sees the light of God's glory upon us. It's fascinating to some. Others follow us trying to put out the light, but they cannot. It's an insane type of warfare that occurs when one decides to uphold God's covenant. Regardless of what the devil sends, we go forth without fear, knowing that we have covenant protection. We need not fear the enemy. Those *in liege* with the enemy should fear what God will do to them for seeking to harm us. Nevertheless, God was doing miraculous things while moving me from place to place. The Holy Spirit explained why that was the case. He said that **"Jesus always did His greatest miracles while on His way somewhere else."** That warmed my heart. So with every detour the Lord sent me on, I began declaring great miracles in that place and God got honor in every city.

In hindsight, it was all was about obtaining my inheritance. Wherever God sent me, He had me taking down principalities over regions and taking territory for the Kingdom. At the same time, the Lord would identify properties, lands and companies He had given to me. Like the Bible said, *"Every place whereon the soles of your feet shall tread shall be yours* (Deuteronomy 11:24)." These are just some of the benefits of being in the right place, at the right time, doing the right thing and walking in covenant with Almighty God. This is also the new covenant walk of faith. Things were simple in Adam's day. He had everything given to him by God. After sin, mankind has had to battle for survival without God. Sure, there were other covenants God made with men, but they had to go into enemy territory and **"fight to take back"** their inheritance in the earth. The same is true for new covenant believers under Jesus Christ.

God's covenant is about restoring everything that had been stolen because of Adam's original sin. The covenant includes everything we would need of while in pursuit of our righteous place in God's Kingdom. In some cases, we are required to confront the devil head on. It takes boldness, but God's got us covered. If He is sending us, His angel will go before us and take out the enemy (Exodus 23:23), so that we can recover all that God says is ours. God's desire is that we be *"made whole."* The plan of salvation is *"to make us whole;"* restoring us back to our ordained positions as sons and daughter of Almighty God. This is a status in earth that treats every believer, **"as if sin had never happened."** The Bible says that we all have sinned and come short of the glory of God (Romans 3:23). It was Jesus Christ who redeemed us back for God's glory. The debt we owed because of sin was nailed to His cross (Colossians 2:14-15). Jesus took our penalty upon Himself. What we owed was *"expunged"* from our record. With a clean record, we are free to move forward to receive our inheritance, which includes not only what the enemy took from our families while we were in sin, but it also includes recompense. That devil has to compensate us for what we have suffered. This is legal jargon because God's covenant is a legal document that is being upheld both in Heaven and in the earth. The Courts of Heaven have ruled in our favor and the reward has been determined. The rest is up to us. We must claim what is ours and go get it.

This is not the typical gospel message that is being preached. What I have shared is Biblical, but the explanations came by revelation. It was the Lord who took me back to Genesis to explain His purpose for mankind. While the world is claiming lack and shortages, God is speaking *"abundance."* There are some Christians who are unsettled by this gospel. It doesn't line up with their theology. Therefore, they covenant with the world and speak lack and sickness. There will be severe *"consequences"* for turning away from God's covenant to follow after man. Such actions bring about the curse (Jeremiah 17:5). The Bible repeatedly shows that we are in covenant with a God of increase. There is no lack in Him. There is nothing ever lacking in what God creates. Yet mankind was given the command to *"replenish and subdue"* the earth. God obviously knew that there would be some loss of fruitfulness due to some kind of decay or *"predator."* How could man understand what it meant to replenish and subdue when everything in the garden was *"perfectly supplied."* Then things changed. The serpent duped mankind into sin. Everything and everyone became *"twisted"* which is another name for *wicked*. They took the covenant of God and *"bent it to their liking."* It is the same spirit (Ephesians 2:2) that operates in the *"children of disobedience"* today. They don't want to do things God's way. They take His laws, keep what they like and discard the rest. Yet, this is a covenant. If you don't keep the rules, you don't receive the benefits. So, they go their own way and covenant with themselves against what God has said. Like Adam, people want to do their own thing, and they become easy prey for the devil. *"Be sober, be vigilant; because your adversary the devil, as a roaring lion, walketh about, seeking whom he may devour (I Peter 5:8)."*

The Lord reminded me of something I was told by a person who was practicing witchcraft. I asked them why they did it. They responded, "Because it works." Then I asked why they believed that it worked. They answered, "Because nobody does what God says." In other words, when we do our own thing rather than doing what God says, we open the door for the devil to control and manipulate. Here is the other part of that situation. When you <u>do</u> obey God and the enemy cannot manipulate you by witchcraft, that is when they begin cursing you with death. When that fails, they will attempt to curse your family with death. This is the devil's strategy. So what! We have a covenant promise from God against the tactics of the devil. He will curse those who curse us (Genesis 12:3). I have seen God's covenant cause curses to **"boomerang"** on the sender many times. I've seen people loose their minds trying to manipulate other people's minds with witchcraft. You cannot speak death on another and it not boomerang on you. The Bible says, *you shall have what you say*. Death and life are in the power of the tongue (Proverbs 18:21). If you speak death over yourself or others, it will come upon you. Whatever you do to others, God will make happen to you. The law of seedtime and harvest never fails. If you've been speaking evil, even death against another. Repent. Don't be a demon on assignment. Repent and let God Bless your life. Don't let that devil take your life. Repent. Give your life to Jesus Christ.

If you are a believer who is being laden with curses, stand on your covenant. Speak the promise over your life and watch God return that curse to the sender. The Lord is serious when He said, *"Touch not mine anointed, and do my prophets no harm* (Psalm 105:15). Touching us is like touching the apple of God's eye (Zechariah 2:8). Even for the Body of Christ, the curse will fall upon those who fight against the brethren in the faith. Be careful how you treat one another. Jesus said that the world would know us by the love we show for one another (John 13:35). Also, keep your mouth off of the leadership of the Church. Pray for the leaders, but don't take it on yourselves to pass judgment upon them. God is the Judge. Keep your hands clean and your heart pure (Psalm 24:4) at all times or you will face the consequences that are reserved for those who violate the covenant of God. Plus that devil is a legalist. He knows the word too. He is just waiting for you to cross that line into unrighteousness. The devil knows that he cannot stop the faithfulness of God. His only tactic is to **"lure"** us into an action that causes us to violate God's covenant. The devil is a thief and a liar. He has stolen from the people of God and the Lord is commanding us to take it all back. Think about it. What do you do when someone violates a legal document? You take them to court to uphold what is written. That is exactly what God expects from His covenant people. The Bible tells us what is written about our covenant with God. When we have completed what is required of us, we can expect to receive from God in return. However, the enemy had been interfering with the delivery of our goods. It's time to stand on the covenant to war against the devil's tactics. We have the power and the authority to do so. Don't treat the things of God so lightly. Jesus gave us all power both in Heaven and in earth. We are citizens of a powerful Kingdom. God's covenant is meant to invoke the power of the Blessing in our lives. We must stand on the covenant by speaking the word only. That requires that we have more faith in the power of God than in the power of men. I feel led to pause and share an example or two about the *"evil consequences"* of witchcraft.

Years ago, I worked as a telephone prayer minister. One night I took a call from a high ranking witch who was experiencing curses coming upon her family. She wanted Jesus to protect them from death. I asked if she had known that her curses would backfire on her some point. She said that she had never given it a thought. Pause. So, either she didn't know or she didn't care. In any case, repercussions of her actions were never her consideration. Suddenly, it was her time to face the music. In my spirit, I sensed that she wanted to live, but was not willing to let go of the witchcraft. When I asked if she wanted to pray the sinner's prayer, she would not commit. I asked if she would be willing to relinquish her rituals and relics, and her drugs. There was a pause on the line. So, I told her that when she was ready to give up everything, that all she had to do was call on the Name of Jesus with a sincere heart and He would answer her. This woman witnessed curses coming back upon her as an *"evil consequence"* of coming against God's people. She was no fool. This woman knew that Jesus Christ had the power to save her, yet she wasn't ready to commit her life to Him.

Then there was the time a minister friend of mine called to get me to stand in agreement in prayer. The father of a friend of his was dying. The minister wanted me to agree in prayer that the man would live. Out of my spirit I heard, *"No!"* The minister became upset with me. He began talking about the compassion of God who wants people healed. *"But no!"* The Holy Spirit began showing how this man was using witchcraft against the people of God. Death was the *"evil consequence"* that came upon him. Finally, the minister had to admit that he knew what the man was doing. We both agreed in prayer that the man repent and get delivered from witchcraft, and then turn his heart to receive God. I don't recall what happened in this case, but I do know that we prayed that God's will be done in that situation. The Bible says that one day we all will have to appear before God. Some will have to appear sooner rather than later. People talk about a Judgment day, but judgments are happening every day. When the curses you spoke begin happening to you. That's your judgment day. When the scheme you devised for another backfires on you. That's your judgment day. When sickness or death comes upon you suddenly. It very well may be that judgment is knocking at your door. Don't ignore such happenings. Stop and ask, "God, what have I done to bring this situation into my life?" Then, let the Lord lead you to the truth about that situation. Obey whatever He reveals to you. Then walk in that new freedom in Christ.

What goes for individuals, also goes for leaders of government and for all those who are in authority over our lives. Many times, curses come upon us because of what others have spoken, planned or schemed against our lives. It seems unfair, but it is true. Even this morning while praying with another minister about breakthrough in an area of my life, the Lord calls the name of someone I hadn't seen or heard about in almost thirty years. While my friend is praying for me, the Lord brings back to my remembrance words that person said to my face way back then. It was a definite word curse, but I didn't know back then so I didn't take it seriously. However, those words were working in my life because I never cast them down. But I did in that moment He revealed them to me. Then the Lord said that the woman **"was suffering"** because of what she said about me. I prayed for her deliverance so that she could be set free.

Back in the day, I believed the lie that we all quoted when we were kids. You remember the saying, *"Sticks and bones may break my bones, but words will never hurt me."* That is a lie from the pit of hell. Witches use words in the form of incantations to put spells on people, for the express purpose of hurting them. I know adults whose lives have been ruined by words that their elders and teachers have spoken over their lives. That is how I received that woman's words some twenty-nine years ago. Those words had been working against my destiny all this time. I never knew it until today. Still, God was able to lead me to speak the appropriate words to release both of us from the curse that woman put in motion. The woman was a public figure. Likewise, many more leaders in America are about to see a **"boomerang"** of every evil plot and scheme they have devised against the people of God. People tend to go into public office and leadership for their own lust for power. They don't seem to understand that with power comes immense responsibility before God. If we go back to the beginning, God created man and gave him dominion over a garden, *a territory or section of real estate* if you please. It was a region of earth that mankind was given to dominate under the rule and reign of Almighty God. That is why the Bible says, *"Let every soul be subject unto the higher powers. For there is no power but of God: the powers that be are ordained of God* (Romans 13:1)." In our day, men and women swear an oath on the Bible, then rule like heathens who don't believe that God exists. That oath was a covenant made before God and man. Yet, wicked leaders continue to covenant together in order to oppress the people. This was never God's plan. These are rebellious men and women who want to prove that they can **"overrule"** Almighty God. They don't believe He is real. They don't believe His power is real. Here is what they don't know. **"God has a covenant with the United States of America."** No man can change it. However, anyone in the land can stand on it. You don't have to be a Christian. God's covenant is a legal document that has been ratified by the Blood of Jesus. If one knows what part of the covenant is being violated, then we take it to the Courts of Heaven and demand execution. This is done through prayer.

Just last evening, the Lord woke me up around 3am and told me to pray for the leaders of the nation. I prayed according to I Timothy 2:1-2 which says, *"I exhort therefore, that, first of all, supplications, prayers, intercessions, [and] giving of thanks, be made for all men; For kings, and [for] all that are in authority; That we may lead a quiet and peaceable life in all godliness and honesty."* Then I prayed in tongues and let the Holy Spirit pray the perfect will of God for those leaders. Later that morning the Lord shared that because of the evil covenants these leaders have made, many were **"under the influence of the evil one and could not resist him."** The power to resist evil comes from God. *"Submit yourselves therefore to God. Resist the devil, and he will flee from you* (James 4:7)." One cannot covenant with the devil and resist him at the same time. It's not possible. It's like the witch who knew Jesus had the power, but she wasn't quite ready to walk away from her covenant with evil. God could not set her free without her permission. Many of America's leaders are also practicing witchcraft and dark arts. They are about to experience the severe consequences of their actions. Unfortunately, the people under their care will also feel these consequences. However, those who know their covenant will not be harmed. The Blood covenant of Jesus Christ supersedes all other covenants in heaven and in earth. In America, God is contending with the spirit of pharaoh that is ruling in the land. It's a demonic power that objects to God's divine authority over the nation and its people. According to God, the fight is about **"whom America will serve."** Plain and simple, this is a **"turf war."** It's no different than the short-sighted gang warriors in the streets in our major cities. They only see limitations distinguishing the "haves from the have nots." So, they choose to take from those who have, like modern day Robin Hoods. Some are just outright robbing the people like common hoods. They are like their father the devil who comes only to steal, kill and destroy (John 10:10).

Listen, God placed within the heart of every man and woman the desire to acquire happiness and the things that bring us happiness in the earth. However, God never condones stealing or killing to take from others. Yet, there are tyrants and thieves who have covenanted with the devil to take what they want by force. They enslave the people with fear. That's just like the devil. He owns nothing. He has created nothing, yet he continues to steal what rightfully belongs to God's family. It's like the devil told Jesus in the wilderness. *"All this power will I give thee, and the glory of them: for that is delivered unto me; and to whomsoever I will I give it* (Luke 4:6)." This was the thief offering to Jesus, that which already belonged to Him. That devil has been peddling stolen goods ever since Adam fell. These goods are the inheritance that belongs to God's people. The devil is slick. He will try to make you work for something that is already yours. He will steal from you. Then sell it back to you and try to make a profit in the deal. How does the devil get away with it? He's a **"flim flam artist."** I heard that word in my spirit. Never have I used that word in my life, but I heard the Holy Spirit say that about the devil. That devil is a **"copy cat."** He is not a creator. He is a **"perverter"** of what God has already created.

Jesus said that the Kingdom was suffering violence, and the violent take it by force (Matthew 11:12). Of course it is suffering violence. That devil is warring against all that God is doing in the earth. He watched God covenant with mankind and the devil mimicked the same, only under the curse. He has no access to the Blessing, for it is *"The Blessing of the Lord* (Proverbs 10:22)." Like earth, the Blessing belongs to the Lord. The devil cannot Bless. It's not in him to Bless. The Blessing comes from God, WHO IS BLESSED forever (Romans 1:25), Amen. The Blessing is an extension of who God is. Therefore in God's covenant, He offers **"all that He has and all that He is"** to those who would uphold His ways. Perhaps you made a deal with that **"flim flam artist,"** and now you are experiencing the consequences. No worries. Just repent. Tell God you are sorry you did it and don't do it again. You may have also blocked your *"divine destiny"* by entering into an evil covenant. Again, don't fear. Clean it up with God. Even right now, you can say. *"Dear Lord, forgive me for entering into evil covenants. I believe that the Blood of Jesus is <u>the</u> covenant that supersedes all covenants in my life and in the lives of my family. I also declare that all evil covenants in my life are annulled and that every agreement I made, or that was made or spoken on my behalf, with death, hell and the grave, shall not stand according to Isaiah 28:18. This I pray In Jesus' Name. Amen."*

Evil curses lingering after those evil covenants are annulled? No worries. Declare this over your life. *"In the Name of Jesus, I declare that every tree that my Heavenly Father has not planted in me, around and through me, be uprooted now according to Matthew 15:13. That includes every tree planted by the evil one through covenants and curses made by me, and by others on my behalf, even by my elders and ancestors. I want to be free to experience the Blessing of the Lord in its fullness. The Bible says that whom the son sets is free indeed* (John 8:36). *I declare that Jesus has set me free and I am free indeed."* Also safeguard your dreams at night. Now that you are free, the enemy may try to *"creep in"* through a night vision or a dream. Be careful not to sign anything or receiving anything in your sleep unless the Spirit of God tells you to. Don't eat any food given to you in your sleep. Don't accept a ring on your finger, nor sign documents in your sleep. As the Bible says, *"But while men slept, his enemy came and sowed tares among the wheat, and went his way* (Matthew 13:25)." Don't do anything in your sleep that signifies a covenant exchange. Stranger things have happened to trap people unaware.

No matter what the devil does, or how he does it, God has a provision in the covenant that protects and delivers us. I've learned this first hand. The Lord always says to me, **"Remember your covenant."** The Bible contains the words of our covenant. We have both the Old and New Testament scriptures at our disposal. Never mind those who say don't use the Old Testament because we are under a new covenant. Although our covenant is new, the scriptures the Lord gives me to war against the devil have come mostly out of the Old Testament. Apostle Paul wrote, *"All scripture [is] given by inspiration of God, and [is] profitable for doctrine, for reproof, for correction, for instruction in righteousness* (II Timothy 3:16)." So, when the Holy Spirit instructs me to use an Old Testament scripture to war against the devil, I don't argue. I also know that this has been a heavy chapter. It was extremely difficult for me to write as well. I've been through so much, seen so much and experienced so many things about covenants that it was difficult to pair it down to put in terms people could easily understand. I spoke much about witchcraft. That is the prevalent spirit that opposed the Church of Jesus Christ, however, there are other covenants that we have entered that seem harmless, almost too simple to be considered, yet I must include these before I conclude with this chapter.

Recently a friend and I began talking about some of the foolish things we did as children. These things seemed innocent at the time, but later in life we recognized the consequences. Things like performing seances and playing with Ouija boards. I recall little boys even cutting their fingers and touching to become "blood brothers." Even the initiation into fraternal organizations are covenants. As adults many of us have joined secret societies in order to propel our business or political careers. People do these things, unaware that they are also entering into covenants, and that there demon spirits behind the scenes. I'm speaking specifically to Christians who are in covenant with God. Did you ever wonder why the Bible said, *"Be ye not unequally yoked together with unbelievers* (II Corinthians 6:14)?" Most times we have used this as it refers to marriage, but in reality this is about any covenant. Remember that God sees His covenant with Jesus similar to a marriage. It's an eternal bond that cannot be broken. A yoke is something that binds people together. It can even be a covenant for any purpose. If that agreement is not ordained by God, then the parties will be yoked together, but one party or both parties may not be able to move in obedience to God. How can two walk together unless they agree (Amos 3:3)?

We can see the evidence of covenants within the government, politics, in corporations and in the Church. There is a prevalent spirit prevalent in every organization. It binds the people to a common purpose and vision. Therefore, the people will have the same speech, dress and mannerism. There is a common thread, a spirit, or ideology that they willingly possess. This is the power of covenant. The people have united themselves in covenant for a common purpose or belief. Whether it is for or against God, that spirit will rest upon the people who are in agreement. It was covenant that cause God's people to erect the Tower of Babel in the Bible. After the flood of Noah's day, God made covenant with Noah and his sons. God Blessed them like He did Adam, and told them to take that Blessing to the uttermost parts of the earth. One son obeyed. The others decided to do their own thing. *"And they said, Go to, let us build us a city and a tower, whose top [may reach] unto heaven; and let us make us a name, lest we be scattered abroad upon the face of the whole earth (Genesis 11:4)."* Here was God's response to what the people had done. *"And the LORD said, Behold, the people [is] one, and they have all one language; and this they begin to do: and now nothing will be restrained from them, which they have imagined to do. Go to, let us go down, and there confound their language, that they may not understand one another's speech. So the LORD scattered them abroad from thence upon the face of all the earth: and they left off to build the city (Genesis 11:6-8)."*

The people were *"one,"* which indicates a covenant, even a covenant that was against God's will. Yet, the Lord said, even in an evil covenant, if the people are *"one," "nothing will be restrained from them which they have imagined to do."* Again, this is the power of covenants. This is also why that devil tries to create discord among brethren in the Body of Christ. He also likes to create strife and envy in families, all for one purpose; to keep people who are supposed to be in covenant, from becoming *"one"* in spirit. We also saw this when God's people were delivered out of slavery in Egypt. They were on their way to the promised land. They sent out spies to verify that the land was what God told them. They sent out twelve spies. Ten came back with an evil report and all of the people believed their report. Only two, Joshua and Caleb agreed with God that they could take the land. They had a *"another [different] spirit."* Those with the evil report ended up dead in the wilderness. Only Joshua, Caleb and those alive with them, went up and possessed the land (Numbers 13:16-33; 14:1-45). Those who argued with God in the wilderness ended up dying there because their spirit was against God.

Covenants have consequences, some bad, some good. We saw the power of covenant in those of the New Testament church. The Bible states in numerous verses that they were in *"one accord (Acts 1:14; 2:1, 46; 4:24; 5:12; 8:6; 15:25)."* That first church was heavily persecuted by enemies who were also in *"one accord (Acts 7:57; 12:20; 18:12; 19:29)"* against them. Still, the scripture emphasizes that the believers of the first Church were *"of one heart and one soul"* and they had *"all things common (Acts 4:32)."* There are **"no one sided covenants."** People (both good and evil) make different kinds of covenants. Ultimately, the parties must be in agreement for the covenant to manifest in power. Let me be clear. God will not force anyone into covenant. He gives people a choice. The only people who attempt to force others into a covenant are those who are on the side of evil. It's the devil who forces people against their will. Some have been forced into covenants under duress. Those covenants are evil and can be broken with the power of God. Again, the Lord gives us a choice of whom we will serve.

Let me stop here to address this matter of choice. There is much rhetoric about people who want a *"choice"* when it comes to abortion. In the eyes of God women want the right to kill. Some would argue that they should have that choice. However according to God this is *"shedding innocent blood."* This is murder and against the covenant that God put in the earth. *"Whoever sheds man's blood, By man his blood shall be shed; For in the image of God He made man* (Genesis 9:6)." While so many Americans are fighting for abortion, the Lord gave insight into the real issue in the nation. He said that **"Americans have no regards for human life."**[1] This should not be said of those who call themselves Christians, but alas it is the same in the Church. How can one make covenant with God to receive eternal life and yet conspire take a human life? If that describes your situation, repent right here and now. God won't condemn you. His desire is that you turn your hearts back to Him. So repent and get back on track with God.

Please understand that God created us for His glory. When He sends a human spirit into the earth, it is for a specific purpose. It doesn't matter how one gets here. Every human born into the earth with a divine purpose that provides a solution that his or her generation needs. Think about how many inventors, artist or humanitarians may have been aborted. Every life matters to God, especially those of the unborn and children. They are precious to the Lord. It's disturbing that many demonic covenants require the sacrifice of the innocent. This is an abomination to God. *"And they served their idols: which were a snare unto them. Yea, they sacrificed their sons and their daughters unto devils, And shed innocent blood, [even] the blood of their sons and of their daughters, whom they sacrificed unto the idols of Canaan: and the land was polluted with blood* (Psalm 106:36-38)." America is polluted with blood of the innocent through abortion and the penalty for those deaths must be paid. The Bible tells how the blood of the innocent speaks and brings a case against their murderers before God. *"The voice of thy brother's blood crieth unto me from the ground* (Genesis 4:10)." In Heaven, there are also souls of those who were killed for their testimony of Jesus Christ saying, *"How long, O Lord, holy and true, doest thou not judge and avenge our blood on them that dwell on the earth* (Revelation 6:10)?" To go

---

1   Matthews, Paula. "The Spirit Of Pharaoh Must Die!." *The War Journal (2011-2020) Volume III*. Atlanta: Spirit & Life Publications[SM], 2020. 141. Print.

even deeper spiritually, I must share a *vision* that the Lord gave me recently about America. *I was awaken in the wee hours of the morning to pray in the spirit. As I prayed, my eyes were opened to see what appeared to be the Spirit of Baal in a vision. He had a monstrous face. There was fire in his mouth. An infant was being placed in his mouth. When I prayed, he disappeared. He vanished. Moments later he appeared again, continuing to devour babies. It was as though he could not be stopped. Someone in authority over our nation had given this demonic entity license to kill our babies. That demon was given authority over America by covenant with our leaders. I kept praying, and witnessed that the spirit of Baal had disappeared, never to return as the ruling spirit over America.* Men in power made a covenant with idols in order to win an election in a nation that is covenanted with The Almighty. Yet, God made it clear. **"The works of man has ended. It is My time," says God.** Therefore, we find ourselves in a showdown similar to when the prophet Elijah went up against the prophets of Baal. God is saying to the people, *"How long halt ye between two opinions? If the LORD be God, follow him: but if Baal, then follow him* (I Kings 18:21)." Evil men want power, so they reach for the supernatural to extend their human power in this earth.

Mankind was created to be **"a spiritual extension"** of Almighty God in covenant. However, when man turned away from His Creator, the human soul was left with a void that only God could fill. When Adam sinned, mankind fell from being a **"god-man"** to becoming man void of God. Today, scientist are attempting to fill that void with computerized chips inside of the human body. They hope to create a mutated being that is unresponsive to God. Really? Such a being could never exist. If God can make a rock to cry out (Luke 19:40), certainly He can do the same with a human-bot of any kind. God can certainly scramble or override a chip because it is man made. Didn't God say **"the works of man have ended?"** What is a chip? What is a bot when it comes to Almighty God? *"The LORD bringeth the counsel of the heathen to nought: he maketh the devices of the people of none effect. (Psalm 33:10)"* Selah.

We are beginning to wind up our discussion on the **"consequences"** of covenants. Adam fell from covenant with God, all of humanity suffers. That which man was supposed to dominate, took dominion over man. It is common to hear of powerful and learned men and women who have fallen under the power of drugs, alcohol, sex, and all kinds of evil influences. These are some of the consequences of covenanting with the kingdom darkness.

The devil has them trapped, holding their sorted secrets over their heads while demeaning them even more. There are many *"political pawns"* in government who will do all the dirty work just so that their twisted secrets are not exposed. *"Black mail and threats are the devil's power tools of the trade."* If you are one who is caught in such a trap, repent right now. Ask God to help you get out. It's just that simple.

These things happen because we turn the truth of God into a lie, and worship and serve *"the creature more than the Creator* (Romans 1:25)."* Men worship demons of debauchery, and find themselves advancing far below God's standard of excellence. Yet, people tend to praise those who fail morally and demean those who attain high moral standards. It's as if human beings have lost their way. This is a *"loser mentality,"* with delusions of grandeur. Men are choosing to serve gods that bring them down to the level of a conniving serpent? Where is the image of God? Where is the likeness of God? The devil is laughing at God as he demeans men and women of influence. He is rubbing it in God's face that the human He created is so weak, that they can be influenced to crawl on their bellies like a snake. This is the "consequence" of turning away from the Most High God to serve low level devils. Beloved, we are about to see fire fall from Heaven and consume evil altars. Just like in Elijah's day, the people will see it, they will fall to their faces crying, *"The LORD, he [is] the God; the LORD, he [is] the God* (I Kings 18:38-39)."

Throughout history, demon possessed men have tried to overthrow Almighty God. They even built altars to connect with the supernatural world, but couldn't reach high enough to reach the True and Living God. It reminds me of what happened in Noah's day. God commanded Noah to build an ark. *"And behold, I, even I, do bring a flood of waters upon the earth, to destroy all flesh, wherein is the breath of life, from under the heaven; and every thing that is in the earth shall die. But with thee will I establish my covenant; and thou shalt come into the ark, thou, and thy sons, and thy wife, and thy son's wives with thee* (Genesis 6:17)." Men had become so evil that God decided to destroy *all flesh*, but spared Noah and his family to start over with a righteous seed. He commanded Noah to take into the ark, two of every sort of animal, male and female. Then the Lord sent the flood and every living being that was upon the face of the earth was destroyed, both man and beast. Noah and his family, and the animals that were in the ark with them remained alive (Genesis 7:12-24). When the flood came, it was too late for people to get aboard. They died in the flood. After the waters subsided, Noah' left the ark and built an altar to the Lord. He took every clean beast and fowl and offered burnt offering on that altar. *"And the Lord smelled a sweet savour (Genesis 8:21)."* This is the covenant that God made with Noah and his sons. *"And I will establish my covenant with you; neither shall all flesh be cut off any more by the waters of a flood; neither shall there any more be a flood to destroy the earth (Genesis 9:11)."*

After Noah, God chose Abraham and made covenant with him saying, *"Get thee out of thy country, and from thy kindred, and from thy father's house, unto a land that I will shew thee (Genesis 12:1)."* Abraham had to leave that which he could see, to follow after a covenant promise that he could not see with his naked eye. God chose Abraham, a old man whose body was about dead, whose wife was barren and beyond child bearing age. He covenanted to make him a great nation. Today, many people both Jews and Arabs alike, call themselves the sons of Abraham. This is their heritage in God. Then God chose Jesus Christ, the seed of Abraham, who would make many of us the partakers of the same promise.

God's love for humanity is truly amazing. One man's sin never had the power to change God's plan for mankind. He had a plan in place to redeem us from sin, even before the worlds were formed. God did this in order that He might seek and find the family He desired in this earth. This is the power of the covenant God made with His Son Jesus on our behalf. Before God formed the man from the dust of the earth, He looked into our future and saw all of our sins. Not only did God see, but like a loving Father, He prepared a way for us to come back and reconcile with Him. What other god has taken away our sins? What other god has given us back our inheritance in this earth? What other god has sacrificed His Own Life to restore humanity back to Himself? I quote the words of Almighty God about Himself. *"Is there a God beside me? Yea, there is no God; I know not any (Isaiah 44:8)."*

JESUS GAVE US POWER

The Kingdom, Power And Glory Returns

No other god, but Jesus Christ has the power to destroy evil curses. *"For this purpose the Son of God was manifested, that he might destroy the works of the devil* (I John 3:8)." Jesus came into the world for the sole purpose of destroying [deeming unlawful and overturning] all the works of the devil since the time of Adam. This was a **"legal Kingdom move"** in the realm of the spirit; a **"class action suit"** file by Heaven against the kingdom of darkness. This case was filed for the benefit of all humanity, which includes complete restoration of that which was lost, along with *"damages"* for what was suffered throughout the generations since Adam. The Bible calls this *recompense*. This is good news for those who desire to be free from the bondage of evil. Anyone who receives Jesus as Lord is eligible for these benefits.

What you've just read is how the Holy Spirit described salvation. It's not just about getting saved from going to hell. It's about mankind being restored back to God's original position for their lives, *"that they may receive forgiveness of sins and inheritance* (Acts 26:18)." The American view of Christianity teaches that Jesus died to take away our sins. That is usually where the gospel message ends, but what Jesus did was much more than that. Forgiveness of sins is just the beginning of the restoration plan God has for mankind.

Sure, Jesus died on the cross taking upon Himself the penalty for our sins. But, when He arose from the dead, Jesus took away from the devil, the power over death, hell and the grave. *"I am he that liveth, and was dead; and, behold, I am alive for evermore, Amen; and have the keys of hell and of death* (Revelation 1:18)." Not only did Jesus resurrect with all power in heaven and in earth, but He turned around and gave that power back to believers. That's why we have been given the great commission to go into all the world and teach all nations (Matthew 28:19). The Kingdom comes with good news for humanity. Jesus' resurrection opened the door for people to return in power as sons and daughters of God. We no longer have to be in bondage to fear of death. Salvation changes the status of our being forever, through the Spirit of adoption (Romans 8:15). As born again descendants of God, we have been given, not only power, but privileges in both Heaven and in earth. And, we don't have to wait to go to Heaven to enjoy these benefits. We have an inheritance that can be used right here on earth. There are both physical and spiritual benefits restored to us as children of God in this earth. According to the Lord, all legal proceeds for the physical goods *"are being held in receivership,"* until the people of God claim what is rightfully theirs.[1] Most of what I have shared may be hard for some to believe, but it's all been documented in the Bible. The details are part of the mysteries the Holy Spirit will reveal to each of us as we diligently seek the Lord for His call and destiny for our lives.

In the meantime, we will focus on the power we have been given through Jesus Christ. When the Lord explained this to me in legal terms, it made sense to me. What Jesus did by coming to earth, preaching and demonstrating the power of the Kingdom, was to **"whet the appetites"** of those who were expecting the Messiah to come and overtake the powers of the rulers of this world. The prophets of old had spoken the word of God concerning Jesus hundreds of years before His arrival. Then came Jesus, the word manifested in flesh. *"And the Word was made flesh, and dwelt among us, (and we beheld his glory, the glory as of the only begotten of the Father,) full of grace and truth* (John 1:14)." Jesus came in the glory of His Father, preaching only one thing in His earthly ministry. *"Repent, for the Kingdom of heaven is at hand* (Matthew 4:17)." What was Jesus saying? To whom was He speaking? Jesus' message was addressed to the Jews; to those who were familiar with the scriptures about the Kingdom. The word Jesus preached was to exhort the people to repent and turn back to God. Sure, they had religion, but where was their faith in God? Where was their faith in His miraculous power to deliver them from the tyranny of Rome? The people were in bondage to a government that had no respect for their religion. Therefore it was easier for many church leaders to make alliances with corrupt government officials in order to further their own positions.

It was in this context that Jesus came preaching about the Kingdom of Heaven being near. The people expected the Messiah, Son of God to appear in Heaven's glory, but not looking like Jesus, the carpenter' son. Nevertheless, the Bible mentions how God *"anointed"* Jesus Christ *"with the Holy Ghost and power,"* which enabled Him to go about *"doing good and healing all"* who were oppressed by the devil (Acts 10:38). Jesus was anointed to preach the Kingdom and demonstrate its power to do good and destroy all

---

[1] Matthews, Paula. "Kingdom Battle Lines Are Drawn."*The War Journal (2011-2020) Volume III*. Atlanta: Spirit & Life Publication[SM], 2020. 104. Print.

the works of the devil. Hang on now. Jesus did this not only to demonstrate the power of God over that of the enemy. Jesus gave us an example to follow as believers. Jesus taught that the word of God had power to destroy anything that the devil had put on mankind. The Bible says that, *"Jesus went about all Galilee, teaching in their synagogues, and preaching the gospel of the kingdom, and healing all manner of sickness and all manner of disease among the people."* As if that were not good enough, the Bible continues. *"And his fame went throughout all Syria: and they brought unto him all sick people that were taken with divers diseases and torments, and those which were possessed with devils, and those which were lunatick, and those that had the palsy; and he healed them* (Matthews 4:23-24)."

This was the example Jesus gave to His disciples. How do we know? Jesus began sending them out to do the same thing. *"And when he had called unto him his twelve disciples, he gave them power against unclean spirits, to cast them out, and to heal all manner of sickness and all manner of disease* (Matthew 10:1)." That's not all. Then Jesus appointed seventy more and sent them out on the same mission. *"And into whatsoever city ye enter, and they receive you, eat such things as are set before you: And heal the sick that are therein, and say unto them, The kingdom of God is come nigh unto you. But into whatsoever city ye enter, and they receive you not, go your ways out into the streets of the same, and say, Even the very dust of your city, which cleaveth on us, we do wipe off against you: notwithstanding be ye sure of this, that the kingdom of God is come nigh unto you* (Luke 10:8-11)." Are you still there? Jesus established a pattern for every believer. When the seventy came back they said, *"Lord, even the devils are subject unto us through they name* (Luke 10:17)." Jesus said to the seventy, *"I beheld Satan as lightning fall from heaven. Behold, I give unto you power to tread on serpents and scorpions, and over all the power of the enemy: and nothing shall by any means hurt you* (Luke 17:18-19)."

In other words, Jesus was saying that the kingdom of darkness lost its power when satan was exiled from heaven. That devil fell to earth, back under the dominion of men anointed and appointed by God to use the Name of Jesus. The disciples were unsaved men. They were not filled with the Holy Ghost as we are today. Jesus had not yet gone to the cross. He hadn't resurrected from the grave, and yet He gave ordinary men the power to use His name to cast out demons. This is the authority every believer has in the Name of Jesus. These men were under the old covenant. Today we have a much better covenant. Still few "believers" really believe that we have power in Jesus' Name to heal and deliver as the Bible says. *"And these signs shall follow them that believe; In my name shall they cast out devils; they shall speak with new tongues; They shall take up serpents; and if they drink any deadly thing, it shall not hurt them; they shall lay hands on the sick, and they shall recover* (Mark 16:17-18)." This is the authority that has been given to every believer in Jesus Christ, to overturn and *"subdue"* all the works of the devil. This also brings mankind back under the Blessing that God spoke over Adam. This is the purpose for teaching and demonstrating the Kingdom, with signs of God's intent to restore us back to the power and glory that was originally given to man. God's people needed to have hope and expectation that the words of the prophets would come to pass. Jesus gave the people hope that the Kingdom would soon appear.

Casting out devils and healing the sick were signs of the power of God's Kingdom; a kingdom that had not yet appeared in the earth. How was it that mere men, followers of the teachings of Jesus Christ, were able to exhibit the power of such a Kingdom? This was and continues to be the mystery of faith. Jesus taught, *"The kingdom of God cometh not with observation: Neither shall they say, Lo here! Or, lo there! For, behold, the kingdom of God is within you* (Luke 17:20-21)." Since salvation in the form of Jesus' sacrifice had not yet come, how could the kingdom of God be within unsaved people? It's not like it is with the new covenant believers in which the Holy Spirit of God resides. Therefore, the kingdom was within their hearts by faith in what the prophets had taught over the generations. Jesus came to rekindle those hearts with confirmation that the Kingdom closer to them than ever before. This was very good news for those who were anticipating the arrival of God's Kingdom.

Jesus, the Messiah King of the Jews, came preaching with evidence that His Kingdom was being restored in the earth. As new covenant believers, we have not been taught about the Kingdom of God. We never understood that Jesus came preaching as the King of the Jews. This was the charge that was laid against Him and got Him executed for treason against Rome. This was not only about our sins as we had been taught. This was about God's Kingdom taking back dominion in this earth. We never understood that when Adam sinned, it meant that he "abdicated" the throne of God's Kingdom in the earth. Not only that, but Adam lost the Kingdom to a low level creeping being. This was a *"coup d'etat,"* an illegal seizure of the earth, its people and possessions, all of which belonged to God (Psalm 24:1). Imagine this. God created everything for His glory. Then He created the man to manage earth's creations. Adam was more than a manager. The earth was more than a garden. It was the garden of God, the center of God's earthly reign. It was God's Kingdom manifested in planet earth, with all its wealth, beauty, power and glory. Satan was also there. *"Thou hast been in Eden the garden of God; every precious stone [was] thy covering, the sardius, topaz, and the diamond, the beryl, the onyx, and the jasper, the sapphire, the emerald, and the carbuncle, and gold: the workmanship of thy tabrets and of thy pipes was prepared in thee in the day that thou wast created (Ezekiel 28:13)."* That garden was under the sovereign rule of Heaven, as was the entire planet. God appoint Adam as king of His Kingdom, and crowned him with glory and honor. God made him to have dominion over all the works of His Hands; and put all things under his feet (Psalm 8:5-6). While you are imagining what God endowed Adam with in the beginning, I want you to begin imagining how Jesus has restored all of this back to you, the new covenant believer. Let's continue.

The Bible does not reveal the details of Adam's Kingdom rule, however, we do know that all things were under his authority. This parallels what God gave to Jesus, who is called the *"last Adam* (I Corinthians 15:45)." The Bible talks about how God put all things under Jesus' feet (Ephesians 1:22). God also made Jesus heir of the world, even though the worlds were made by Him (Hebrews 1:2). Although Jesus is considered the last Adam, He carries considerably more honor and glory since He was also with the Father before Adam was born. As the Bible says, *"In the beginning was the Word, and the Word was with God, and the Word was God. The same was in the beginning with God. All things were made by him; and without him was not any thing made that was made (John 1:1-3)."*

As co-creator with the Father of everything in creation, Jesus has a vested interest in what happens in this earth. He is the *"Alpha and Omega, the beginning and the end, the first and the last (Revelation 22:13)."* Nothing was made without Him, and all things were made by Him. Jesus and the Father designed the blueprint of the earth and how it was to operate as a territory of Heaven. It was always meant to be part of God's domain, since He is Eternal King (I Timothy 1:17). Planet earth was to be under the dominion of the sons and daughters of God. That is why God appointed Jesus, His only begotten son, to be King over God's earthly Kingdom. This is also why

Jesus came, to restore our positions of sons and daughters of God in this earth. He was the *"firstborn among many brethren* (Romans 8:29)." This restoration came to the Jews first, but ultimate it would extend to all the people of the earth. Jesus was the prophesied to be Messiah King, not only of the Jews, but also of the Gentiles. *"Of the increase of [his] government and peace [there shall be] no end, upon the throne of David, and upon his kingdom, to order it, and to establish it with judgment and with justice from henceforth even for ever. The zeal of the LORD of hosts will perform this* (Isaiah 9:7)." In this manner would all nations be reunited under God's Kingdom like it would have been from the beginning. God's plan for salvation was much more than about Heaven. It was about restoring Heaven upon the earth. It's about restoring God's Heavenly Kingdom in all of its power and glory back into the hands of mankind. This is what Jesus did for us. Therefore, it's more than Heaven. It's bigger than Church. This is Kingdom!

Take a closer look at how the Bible is worded throughout. You will find Kingdom speech from Genesis to Revelation. God's people are called a *"royal priesthood* (1 Peter 2:9)." Jesus Christ washed us from our sins and made us to be *"kings and priests unto our God* (Revelation 1:6)." Jesus is the King of kings. We, the Body of Christ are the kings of over whom Jesus reigns. Every aspect of our salvation is related to reestablishing God's Kingdom in the earth. *"For if by one man's offence death reigned by one; much more they which receive abundance of grace and of the gift of righteousness shall reign in life by one, Jesus Christ* (Romans 5:17)." Therefore, when we say that Jesus came to earth to overturn the works of the devil, this was a **"legal maneuver"** that was required to restore God's Kingdom in the earth. This is not the typical salvation message that is being preached, but it is what the Lord taught me and told me to teach; **"the Kingdom."**

It's been almost a dozen years ago since the Lord first said to me that He was **"Restoring An Ancient Kingdom Dynasty"** in the earth. God spoke to me using the word **"Dynasty"** referring to a generation of His sons and daughters ruling in the earth. This is why God Blessed Adam. This is why Jesus returned the Blessing to us. **"The Blessing is our royal scepter."** With it, we rule and reign righteously on the earth. Jesus came to restore God's Kingdom, its power and glory in the earth, so that we could rule and reign in His Name. The Bible says that God chose us in Him before the foundation of the world and *"Blessed us with all spiritual blessings in the heavenly places in Christ* (Ephesians 1:3-4)." We were called by God, according to His purpose and *"predestined to be conformed to the image of His Son* (Romans 8:28-29)." In short, God chose us just so that we could be a *"clone"* of His Son Jesus Christ. Now, of course, we come from different backgrounds and experiences that shape our humanity, but spiritually the born again spirit is *"pre-wired"* to be like Jesus Christ. It's in our spiritual DNA. Therefore our spirits have been programmed to evolve into dynastic rulers in God's Kingdom. This placing within the spirits of born again men and women, that which *"re-creates"* us back into the image and likeness of God. Thus we are called the *"new creature"* in Christ. *"Therefore, is any man be in Christ, he is a new creature: old things are passed away; behold, all things are become new* (II Corinthians 5:17)." Through this *"new creature"* God is able to uphold His dominion over the earth as it was in Adam's day.

This is not the typical salvation message. It is the Kingdom message the Lord gave me to preach. It's Biblical and prophetic in nature. The thing to focus on is our new authority in Christ over the kingdom of darkness. When Adam fell, satan became *"god"* of this world (II Corinthians 4:4). He was never able to exalt his throne above God, even though that was his plan when he deceived Adam out of his inheritance. Satan wasn't even able to reign as king like Adam did. He was a serpent, cursed to crawl on his belly and eat dust all the days of his life (Genesis 3:14). He could never be king over the human. They were above his status. Only human beings were permitted to operate in this earth. God alone gave dominion to mankind. Satan was of a different kind. He was *"more subtil than any beast of the field* (Genesis 3:1)." He was still considered a beast. How could a *"creeping thing"* rule over man and take dominion away from God's Kingdom?

Consider what he did to Adam. He deceived the man by having him question what God said. This had been so successful that the devil has used it on mankind ever since Adam. However, the highest status the devil could achieve was *"prince."* That devil, will never become king. He does not have that authority. When he was kicked out of Heaven, the highest position he could expect was *"prince of this world."* He has also been called *"the prince of the power of the air, the spirit that now worketh in the children of disobedience* (Ephesians 2:2)." Another way to look at, satan is the principal spirit behind the demons spirits that operate in the atmosphere between the sky and the earth. Even so, Jesus went to the cross and took that title away from the devil too. *"Now is the judgment of this world: now shall the prince of this world be cast out* (John 12:31)."

Indeed, Jesus came to earth to destroy every work of the devil since the time of Adam. By then the curse had pervaded the earth. The only way Jesus could totally defeat satan was to destroy the power of the curse and the death that it brought upon mankind. There was only one way to do it. Jesus had to become a curse and die in order to overcome its power to destroy us. In doing so, Jesus would set a *"spiritual precedent"* for His Body. In order to take the power of a thing, we must take it on and strip it of its power.

Think about it. Even before He went to the cross, Jesus was exercising full authority over the enemy. That is why He could send out the twelve and then the seventy in His same power and authority. It was understood that they could heal the sick, cleanse the lepers, raise the dead, and cast out devils, because *freely they received* from Jesus and freely they could give what they received to others (Matthew 10:8). Could this be the problem in the Church today? Could it be that we see no signs, wonders or miracles are being performed because the Body of Christ never received freely from the Lord? Perhaps it is. Surely, if we had freely received it would be such a joy to extend that same freedom and relief to others. These were unsaved men performing miracles in Jesus' Name! The demons were indeed subject to unsaved men. That authority God originally gave mankind *"replenish and subdue"* was being demonstrated, but Jesus didn't stop there. It's one thing to heal, deliver and make people whole after what the devil did to them. It's yet another to go into hell and resurrect with all power both in heaven and in earth (Matthews 28:18).

Let's think of this in terms we understand in our modern world. It's one thing to stop crime on the streets by putting the criminals behind bars and having them make restitution. It's yet another to locate the "kingpin" or the "crime bosses" behind the operations and shutting the whole thing down. That's what Jesus did to satan when He died on the cross. He descended into hell, overthrew its power and arose from the grave. The Bible says of Jesus, *"Having disarmed principalities and powers, He made a public spectacle of them, triumphing over them in it* (Colossians 2:15)." Jesus *"disarmed"* the powers of darkness who controlled the entire curse-death-hell operation. Can you imagine satan and his demons being paraded in the streets in handcuffs? This all while Jesus, the conquering hero rides in declaring, *"All power is given unto me in heaven and in earth. Go ye therefore, and teach all nations, baptizing them in the name of the Father, and of the Son, and of the Holy Ghost: Teaching them to observe all things whatsoever I have com-*

manded you: and, lo, I am with you alway, [even] unto the end of the world. Amen (Matthew 28:18-20)." Now, I ask. Who was Jesus talking to? Who was He commanding to go and teach the nations? For years, I was told that it was only for the twelve disciples of Jesus' day. Really? Then what should the remaining Christians do in their life time? Sit around and wait for Jesus to return so we can get up out of here? No! No! No! We cannot sit around when there is work to be done in the earth. God didn't send Jesus to do what He did just so we could do nothing.

The Bible says that Jesus died for all so *"that they which live should not henceforth live unto themselves, but unto him which died for them, and rose again."* Jesus gave His life and we are expected to give our lives back to God. We are indeed new creatures as it is written, *"old things are passed away: behold, all things are become new. And all things are of God* (II Corinthians 5:15, 17-18)." What old things have passed away? That old way of living and that old way of thinking cannot longer operated in God's new creation. Remember how God created us for His purpose; *". . . his workmanship, created in Christ Jesus unto good works . . (Ephesians 2:10)."*

Listen, this is why Jesus conquered all of the power of the enemy and gave it back to God's people. No other god, nor idol claims to have come into the earth for this purpose. Think about it. God left Heaven, and was born in the earth, in the form of a man and conquered all the power of the devil. Why a man? Jesus had to come as a man because God gave mankind authority in the earth. It was a man, the son of God, who forfeited his throne on earth. It could have only been a man of Adam's kin, who could come with Heaven's authority to reign on the throne of God's Kingdom. Jesus also came as our example to follow as sons and daughters of God. I'll never forget the day that the Father came to me saying, **"Paula, are you ready to become a son?"**[2] Now for you all who are hung up on gender, hold on. In God's Kingdom, a son is not a gender. It's a title of honor for those who are walking in maturity in the things of God. As the Bible says, *"For as many as are led by the Spirit of God, they are the sons of God* (Romans 8:14)." Whoever receives Jesus Christ is given the authority as a son of God (John 1:12). However, only those who walk in obedience to the Spirit of God will reap the benefits of sonship. The Father taught me much about sonship. He said that it was about living like Jesus. He was our example to follow. God told me to read the red letters in the New Testament, paying particular attention to what

---

2   Matthews, Paula. "Blossoming Into Sonship." *Taught By God*. Atlanta: Spirit & Life Publications^{SM}, 2021. 45-46. Print.

Jesus said about saying only what the Father said, and doing whatever the Father told Him to do. Jesus never did anything on His own. He was always obedient to the Father. They were inseparable. They were one. Jesus' prayer for us was that believers would be come one, as He and the Father are one (John 17:23). I thought, "How could I ever be like Jesus? Jesus was god. I'm only human." I had to learn that as new creatures in Christ, we have been injected with God's DNA. Our spirits have become one with the Father. When we are led by the Spirit of God, our minds and bodies will follow suit. The power is within us, The word of God is available to us. The Holy Spirit will guide us. We have all we need to follow in the footsteps of Jesus.

Let's walk through some examples of sonship. Remember that Jesus became a sinner cursed and condemned to die and go to hell. Yet, Jesus was innocent. How could this happen to Him who had no sin? To fulfill His purpose in the earth, Jesus would have to be wrongly accused, illegally tried and convicted as a criminal and sentenced to death. We hear about things like this happening often in our day and age. But, God was purposely sending Jesus to earth to be set up and wrongly accused by a council of men. Jesus had made an agreement with the Father to lay His life down for us. In exchange, Jesus would arise from the dead after three days. Jesus told this to his disciples, but they did not understand. Peter said, *"Be it far from thee, Lord: this shall not be unto thee"* Jesus rebuked him saying, *"Get thee behind me, Satan: thou art an offence unto me: for thou savourest not the things that be of God, but those that be of men* (Matthew 16:22-23)." The disciples had no clue that Jesus was talking by faith.

After Jesus' resurrection, Peter would lead the apostles in understanding why Jesus had to die. *"Ye men of Israel, hear these words; Jesus of Nazareth, a man approved of God among you by miracles and wonders and signs, which God did by him in the midst of you, as ye yourselves also know: Him, being delivered by the determinate counsel and foreknowledge of God, ye have taken, and by wicked hands have crucified and slain: Whom God hath raised up, having loosed the pains of death: because it was not possible that he should be holden of it* (Acts 2:22-24)." In this example, the apostles knew how they were to follow their Master's example of how to live, sacrifice and die (if needed) for the cause of Christ. They went about doing mighty miracles and bringing multitudes to Christ, even in the midst of great persecution and threats of death. Peter wrote: *"Beloved, think it not strange concerning the fiery trial which is to try you, as though some strange thing happened unto you: But rejoice, inasmuch as ye are partakers of Christ's sufferings; that, when his glory shall be revealed, ye may be glad also with exceeding joy . . . .Wherefore let them that suffer according to the will of God commit the keeping of their souls [to him] in well doing, as unto a faithful Creator* (I Peter 4:13-14, 19)."

Peter had learned to follow Jesus perfectly, even to death. Jesus is every believer's example to follow. He had His assignment from the Father. By faith, Jesus had to receive the sins of every human being who would ever live. He took sin into His Spirit, which required that Jesus be separated from His Holy Father (Isaiah 59:2). Jesus had never been separated from the Father. On that cross with all of our sins upon Him, Jesus and the Father no longer one. Our sin spiritually estranged them from one another. *"And about the ninth hour Jesus cried with a loud voice, saying, Eli, Eli, lama sabachthani? That is to say, My God, my God, why hast thou forsaken me* (Matthew 27:46)?" Imagine how it pained the Father to hear such words. He had not forsaken the son, but spiritually it was agonizing for them both. However, Jesus' suffering was not in vain. *"Surely he hath borne our griefs, and carried our sorrows: yet we did esteem him stricken, smitten of God, and afflicted. But he [was] wounded for our transgressions, [he was] bruised for our iniquities: the chastisement of our peace [was] upon him; and with his stripes we are healed* (Isaiah 53:4-5)."

Jesus went to the cross remembering the covenant which He made with His Father on our behalf. He suffered the curse so that we didn't have to. Jesus paid the price so that we could be free from our sins and iniquities. He suffered for our peace and our healing. So how does sonship work? Whatever Jesus suffered for, is what we also strive to receive in this life. Whatever Jesus bore, we should bear no more. Therefore we don't grieve nor sorrow, even at the death of a loved one, especially if they were saved. We know where they are. It's where we all desire to be one day. Sure, we miss them, but we are not to carry grief and sorrow because Jesus bore it for us. *"But I would not have you to be ignorant, brethren, concerning them which are asleep, that ye sorrow not, even as others which have no hope* (I Thessalonians 4:13)." Jesus was wounded and bruised, not for his sins, but for ours. Therefore we should strive against both sin and iniquities. This is why we break evil covenants and curses. This is why we cast out devils and set people free from habitual sins. Many of which can still operate in one who is saved. Salvation is just the beginning. We must be continually cleansed through the washing of water by the word (Ephesians 5:26). If we continue in the word, not just reading it, but endeavoring to live what we read, we will be free indeed. Finally, on that cross Jesus was severely chastened, mocked and scorned in every way possible so that we could receive our peace and be healed. So we strive for the peace of God. We strive for our healing because of what Jesus suffered for us to receive. In Jesus' suffering and death, He was able to destroy *"him that had the power of death, that is, the devil* (Hebrews 2:14)." Notice that the Bible said that the devil *"had"* the power of death. Jesus said of his sacrifice, *"I lay down my life, that I might take it again. No man taketh it from me, but I lay it down of myself. I have power to lay it down, and I have power to take it again. This commandment have I received of my Father* (John 10:17-18)."

Here is the key to sonship. Like Jesus, we must be willing to say, *"Not my will, but thine, be done* (Luke 22:42)." That means giving up our selfish desires, and taking up the promise of the Father. We must decrease so that He may increase (John 3:30) in our lives. Jesus said, *"If any [man] will come after me, let him deny himself, and take up his cross daily, and follow me* (Luke 9:23)." I know this is a lot of scripture, but every believer ought to know the importance of why we must follow after Jesus. Salvation was never about getting us to Heaven. It was about following Jesus' example and demonstrating the Kingdom, its power and glory upon the earth. Jesus commissioned His Church [the Body of Christ] to take up where He left off. We must finish His Kingdom mission in the earth. We'll talk more about this later in this book. For now we will continue talking about the power we have in Christ over the curse.

In this book we are focusing on breaking evil covenants and curses. In these last days, God will be coming down hard upon evil. He doesn't want people to get hurt. So it is imperative for us to sever all ties to the kingdom of darkness. How does this look to you? God loved us so much that He sacrificed Jesus, to be a curse for us, so that we could live in the Blessing. Now, consider the ones who say they believe, but then they make covenant with evil and become entangled again in sin. How do you think that makes God feel? How would you feel if you risked everything to rescue someone from death, and they go right back into that same dangerous situation? You wouldn't be eager to help that person again, unless they were serious about changes in their life. Thank Heaven we are not God. He has mercy towards us, even when we backslide into sin. God extends His grace towards us because He knows we have weaknesses in this flesh. Notwithstanding, Jesus went to the cross for us. His sacrifice should at least demand loyalty from those who believe.

Jesus took the curse upon Himself so that we could experience the same Blessing that God pronounced on Abraham (Galatians 3:13-14). *"Now the LORD had said unto Abram, Get thee out of thy country, and from thy kindred, and from thy father's house, unto a land that I will shew thee: And I will make of thee a great nation, and I will bless thee, and make thy name great; and thou shalt be a blessing: And I will bless them that bless thee, and curse him that curseth thee: and in thee shall all families of the earth be blessed* (Genesis 12:1-3)." Notice the similarity in purpose this Blessing has with that which God spoke over Adam and over Noah and sons. *"Be fruitful, and multiply, and replenish the earth, and subdue it: and have dominion* (Genesis 1:28; 9:1)." Both of these Blessings reveal that God's intent for humanity is to increase us more and more; to make us great in the earth. He also desires that we increase the Blessing throughout the earth. As concerning things that oppose the Blessing, we are to replenish, subdue and have dominion. To Abraham, God gives a provision concerning those who are either for or work against us. It is God's intent to curse those who curse us. Certainly we should never curse ourselves, but the same provision would apply to what we say over our own lives.

What Jesus preached and demonstrated through the gospel of the Kingdom is highly consistent with both the Blessing of Abraham, and that Blessing which was spoken over Adam, and over Noah and his sons. When Jesus came preaching, the people claimed to be the children of Abraham and therefore heirs to his promise. Yet, they were being hindered by the devil. Jesus' first assignment was to come destroy the works of the devil that had afflicted the seed of Abraham. Luke records Jesus coming into the synagogue as was His custom, He stood up to read and was handed the Book of Isaiah. Jesus read these words. *"The Spirit of the Lord [is] upon me, because he hath anointed me to preach the gospel to the poor; he hath sent me to heal the brokenhearted, to preach deliverance to the captives, and recovering of sight to the blind, to set at liberty them that are bruised, To preach the acceptable year of the Lord. And he closed the book, and he gave [it] again to the minister, and sat down. And the eyes of all them that were in the synagogue were fastened on him. And he began to say unto them, This day is this scripture fulfilled in your ears* (Luke 4:16-21)." Jesus came to set the captives free from the power of darkness. They were a Blessed people who were living in bondage to the evil one. Evidently they had grown accustomed to no relief, no healing and no deliverance from demonic influence. Jesus went about healing and setting people free and the religious rulers wanted to have Him killed. Why? Before we answer, let's look at another example that proves God desire is for His people to be free to experience the Blessing of Abraham.

Jesus was preaching in a synagogue and noticed a woman who had a *"spirit of infirmity"* for eighteen years. She was crippled and could not straighten herself up. Jesus said to her, *"Woman, thou art loosed from thine infirmity."* He laid His hands on her and immediately she straightened up and praised God. The religious leaders complained that Jesus had healed on the Sabbath. He responded, *"[Thou] hypocrite, doth not each one of you on the sabbath loose his ox or [his] ass from the stall, and lead [him] away to watering? And ought not this woman, being a daughter of Abraham, whom Satan hath bound, lo, these eighteen years, be loosed from this bond on the sabbath day* (Luke 13:10-16)?" This woman had a covenant right to be healed being the seed of Abraham, yet the religious leaders found fault in Jesus because He violated their "church rules." Jesus was very vocal when it came to leaders who honor the traditions of men instead of the word of God. *"Full well ye reject the commandment of God, that ye may keep your own tradition* (Mark 7:9)."

Herein lies the issue in the Church of Jesus Christ in America. For the most part, it is very similar to the church in Jesus' day. They were happy to know that they were Blessed by God. Yet, they revere man made doctrines and traditions over the word of God. Unfortunately, the Church is ordained to be Blessed, but it operates mostly against the will of God and therefore is cursed (Jeremiah 17:5). Although Jesus redeemed us from the penalty of sin, willful rebellion causes many in the Church to fall right back into sin and the curse. What was the purpose of redemption through Jesus Christ? It was to restore our dominion over the power of darkness; which includes subduing the demonic forces and breaking evil covenants and curses. These are the "good works" we were created to perform. This is why Jesus died. *"Who gave himself for us, that he might redeem us from all iniquity, and purify unto himself a peculiar people, zealous of good works* (Titus 2:14)." Overthrowing the powers of darkness is how we demonstrate our good works in the earth. This may sound intimidating to some, but consider how Jesus lived on the earth. If He is our example to follow, then we should also be opening blind eyes, or raising people from the dead. This is what Jesus did and it was no parlor trick. The people of God were suffering in Jesus' day and they continue to suffer today. The Church of Jesus Christ must demonstrate God's Kingdom power over all of the power of the devil. Jesus was showing us how to *"subdue"* and take *"dominion"* over the darkness by speaking God's word with power. Jesus expects His Church to do even greater works than He did (John 14:12). This will be our part in Restoring God's Kingdom Dynasty in the earth. It's not us, but *Christ in us* doing the work. Our spirits are **"re-created"** at salvation. We became God's *"workmanship, created in Christ Jesus"* to perform good works that were ordained for our lives (Ephesians 2:10). Christ is the anointing (power of God) that is necessary to produce good works in the earth.

We are in covenant with God and His Son Jesus Christ. They did their part of the covenant. Now, it's our turn. Jesus paid the sin penalty so that mankind could be reconciled back to God, but each person must **"cash in"** on that redemption individually. There is only one way to reconcile with God. People don't like to hear it, but it's the truth anyhow. The path to redemption was prepared and orchestrated by God Himself. It is exactly as Jesus said, *"I am the way, the truth, and the life: no man cometh unto the Father, but by me* (John 14:6)." Salvation through Jesus Christ is a free gift for whosoever would believe. What other god is offering forgiveness of sins, and an inheritance (Acts 26:18)? Not one! Jesus came to Bless us by removing our sins, so that we could receive an inheritance in God's Kingdom. Jesus authorized to *"eradicate"* the darkness of this world. All others are counterfeits. Even the devil masquerades as an angel of light (II Corinthians 11:14). His deception works for a while, until the people of the world get tired of the **"flim flam."** Then they will demand the truth. When this happens, the evil hasn't a leg to stand on. He will surely fall, because God's word is truth. Jesus Christ, the word of God, is truth. Consider that truth and you'll find the path to freedom from the darkness.

One must understand that there are only two spiritual powers operating in the earth, that of God and that which comes from satan. What about human power? Sure, people some power, but remember how God created us. We are spirit beings, but our human spirits emanate from one of two spiritual fathers, God, or satan. Only the born again spirit is born of God. At salvation the Spirit of God comes to reside within the believer, **"re-cre-**

ating" the person in the same mold in which Adam was created. However, human beings who erect "their own kingdoms," emulate satan himself. The Bible records what brought Lucifer down to hell. He said in his heart,*"I will ascend into heaven, I will exalt my throne above the stars of God: I will sit also upon the mount of the congregation, in the sides of the north: I will ascend above the heights of the clouds; I will be like the most High. Yet thou shalt be brought down to hell, to the sides of the pit* (Isaiah 14:13-15)." In other words, if you decide to exalt your throne above Almighty God, you will be brought down to hell into the pit. Trust me. You don't want to go to hell, not even for a visit and definitely not for all eternity. Hell was not created for human beings. *"Then shall he say also unto them on the left hand, Depart from me, ye cursed, into everlasting fire, prepared for the devil and his angels* (Matthew 25:41)." Consider this the next time you decide to play **"a game of thrones"** with Almighty God. It will not go well with you.

God chose us to represent Him in this world. That means separating from how the world thinks and renewing our minds to think like God. So far, we have learned His intent to Bless us. We have learned that Jesus returned to us the Kingdom, the power and the glory of God for us to manifest His promise in the earth. To do this, we have the promise of the Spirit (Luke 24:49). It is the gift of the Holy Spirit. More than a gift, the Holy Spirit is power! *"But ye shall receive power, after that the Holy Ghost is come upon you* (Acts 1:8)." What kind of power? The Holy Ghost empowers one to be able to perform the same miracles that Jesus did. The Holy Ghost and power are the promises of God for every believer. Many have been taught not to believe in the Holy Ghost. Yet, He is the third person of the godhead; the Father, the Son, and the Holy Ghost. God sends us the Holy Ghost to teach us all things (John 14:26). The Holy Ghost is also the Spirit of Truth. He will guide us into all truth (John 16:13). Every believer needs to be full of the Holy Ghost and led by the Spirit (Luke 4:1). Otherwise they will continue striving to live the Christian life and it won't be successful; especially not against the works of the devil. The power of the Holy Ghost is needed to break curses off of our lives.

Jesus also gave us the powerful keys of the kingdom of heaven. Keys are **revelation knowledge** from the Holy Spirit that helps us fulfill our Kingdom assignments. These keys **"unlock the mysteries"** associated with our destinies. With these revelatory keys we can bind and loose whatever Heaven desires in this earth. *"Verily I say unto you, Whatsoever ye shall bind on* *earth shall be bound in heaven: and whatsoever ye shall loose on earth shall be loosed in heaven* (Matthew 16:19)." These are keys of Kingdom dominion. The Holy Spirit will reveal the will of the Father for a particular situation. It may be revelation knowledge that seems impossible given the current circumstances. However, God commands us to call those things that be not as though they were (Romans 4:17). Faith speaks what it believes (II Corinthians 4:13). At creation, God saw the earth dark, void and without form (Genesis 1:2). God saw one thing in the earth, but He spoke another thing into existence. *"Let there be light: and there was light* (Genesis 1:3)." God spoke the outcome He desired in the earth. With binding and loosing we do the same. We may see lack in our lives, but the Spirit of God is speaking *"abundance."* We bind up the lack and loose Heaven's abundance in our lives. With these revelatory keys of the Kingdom, we don't speak what we have. We speak the outcome we desire in a situation, and the Father will do the work to bring it to pass. In this way God's Kingdom will come and His will shall be done, in the earth as it is in Heaven.

For years, the Lord has been ministering to me about His Kingdom promises coming to pass in these last days. I've been binding what He commanded me to bind. I loosed what He commanded me to loose. However, some things could only come to pass with prayer and fasting. The more I prayed, the more the Holy Spirit revealed things that were hindering me from receiving the promises of God. After that fast, the Lord gave me a word for His people. It is necessary that we *"walk circumspect"* before the Lord. We are on a narrow path to victory over the adversary. The Lord cautioned us to, **"Be Intentional."** Don't just follow the crowd. Don't just go with the flow of things in this world. **"Be Intentional"** in doing what God wants you to do and say. This will be our protection from the traps of the enemy. He also said that we should **"Pray for one another,"** that we, the Body of Christ should be more intentional to follow after God and not after man. To receive what God has for us, we have to **"let go"** of things that are hindering us from receiving. For every *seed* [word, action, thought, deed], there is a *harvest* [an outcome, whether good or evil]. This is why we need to **"Be Intentional,"** if we want to experience the goodness of God in the land of the living. Think about it. Our enemy, the devil is *very intentional* about not letting up on us. He wants us sick or dead. He wants us poor and suffering. Jesus already suffered those things for us. Therefore, we must strive against sickness, death and suffering. We are appointed for the Blessing and not for the curse.

Here's another thing. We know, that what God has Blessed, no man can curse (Numbers 23:8). Certainly the Blessing of the Lord was instituted at creation and cannot be removed. I heard the Holy Spirit say, **"The Blessing of the Lord stands forever."** Therefore, the Blessing wasn't taken away from humanity. We were separated from it by sin. It was Jesus, who restored us back to the Blessing. Indeed, no man can curse what God has Blessed, but it does not stop the devil from hurling curses at us. As Bible believing saints, we know that *No weapon formed against us shall prosper; and every tongue [that] shall rise against us in judgment we shall condemn.* This is the heritage of the servants of the LORD, and our righteousness is of the LORD (Isaiah 54:17). Weapons are always forming, but we have a covenant promise that gives us power over every weapon of the enemy. We stand on our covenant. We who are heirs of God, and joint heirs with Christ, are Blessed to overthrow, break, and throw down the effect of curses. This is also how we walk in the Blessing. We're to be armed to take down enemy weapons at all times. Our covenant has a special provision that curses those who desire to curse us (Genesis 12:3).

Our assignment is clear. If we want the fullness of the Blessing in our lives, we must **"Be intentional"** in our obedience to God. We must **"be intentional"** in our efforts to take a stand against the evil that is hindering the Blessing in our lives. We have power through Jesus Christ. We have the word of God. We have the Spirit of God to teach and guide us. The prophet of old said it this way. *"And the LORD said unto me, Behold, I have put my words in thy mouth. See, I have this day set thee over the nations and over the kingdoms, to root out, and to pull down, and to destroy, and to throw down, to build, and to plant* (Jeremiah 1:9-10)."

Treading On Serpents And Scorpions

We now know that Jesus gave us power over all the power of the enemy, which includes evil covenants and curses. What remains to be seen is what we do with that power. How do we tread upon serpents and scorpions? What does it mean when Psalm 91:13 says, *"Thou shalt tread upon the lion and adder: the young lion and the dragon shalt thou trample under feet?"* These are demon powers in the realm of the spirit that hinder the Blessing in our lives. How does one tread and trample upon these spirits? Christians sing about the devil being under their feet, but what does that look like in practice? Whether one treads or tramples the enemy, these words imply a physical maneuver that **"utterly destroys and makes ineffective"** the plan of the adversary.

I'm reminded of the time that the Lord showed me the armor He had placed on me for His service. Now, many of us are aware of the roman armor described in the Book of Ephesians. *"Wherefore take unto you the whole armour of God, that ye may be able to withstand in the evil day, and having done all, to stand. Stand therefore, having your loins girt about with truth, and having on the breastplate of righteousness; And your feet shod with the preparation of the gospel of peace; Above all, taking the shield of faith, wherewith ye shall be able to quench all the fiery darts of the wicked. And take the helmet of salvation, and the sword of the Spirit, which is the word of God (Ephesians 6:13-17)."* This is how believers are told to **"suit up"** for battle against the enemy. Well, one day, the Father came to me saying, **"You are about to experience what Jesus felt in hell."** If that wasn't shocking enough, He then revealed my armor for that assignment. It was nothing like what the Bible said. It looked like something out of a science fiction movie. My body was completed covered in what looked like deep tread tire materials, kind of like the Michelin man, but I had deadly spikes embedded in the tread and I knew this was all about hand-to-hand combat. Then the Lord sent me into battle.[1] This was going to be ugly warfare for sure. Listen, no one said that being a Christian was easy. If they did, they lied. Think about this. God asked the **"hard thing"** of Jesus requiring that His Blood be shed in order to buy us back. Because of Jesus' sacrifice, God would not

---

1   Matthews, Paula. "Walking Through The Valley Of The Shadow Of Death." *Jesus Gave Us Power Over Death*. Atlanta: Spirit & Life Publications[SM], 2014. 70-71. Print.

withhold any good thing from us. In the Mind of Christ, it was worth all the suffering if it meant that humanity would be reconciled back to God. The price Jesus paid was significant. He gave His life in order to redeem many lives. All He requires in return is our *"life for a Life."* That is what Jesus gave us. That is what He is asking of us in return. We don't have to die on the cross like He did, but there is a cross (a commitment of faith) we are expected to bear, not just for ourselves, but for our families and loved ones. Jesus gave us His life because the Father loved us so much. Jesus died on the cross because of His love for the Father. *"No greater love hath no man than this, that a man lay down his life for his friends* (John 15:13)." What are we willing to give for those we love? Are we willing to lay down our selfish lives to see a loved one freed from the chains of the enemy? This is the Mind of Christ, to set the captives free.

Jesus didn't just give His life, He took back power from the enemy and gave it back to human beings on earth. This wasn't just a **"take back,"** it was a **"complete restoration"** where the Blessing is the norm and not the exception. Jesus came that we might have that abundant life God ordained for us before the foundation of the world. This was only made possible because Jesus obeyed the Father's commands all the way to the cross. It was on that cross that Jesus fulfilled the word that God spoke over the serpent in the garden. *"And I will put enmity between thee and the woman, and between thy seed and her seed; it shall bruise thy head, and thou shalt bruise his heel* (Genesis 3:15)." Because the serpent deceived mankind in the garden, God punished it by declaring war between the seed of the serpent and the seed of the woman. What's interesting is that God didn't put the seed in the woman. The seed of the human is in the male. Prophetically speaking, the woman in this verse was not just Eve, but the seed of the Virgin Mary, which is Jesus Christ. It also interesting to note that God mentioned that the serpent, aka satan, the devil, would also have seed. Earlier we mentioned that there were two fathers of spirit. God refers to that here in this scripture verse, meaning that there would be hostility between mankind and the devil as long as the earth remains.

This all stands to reason when you consider that satan wanted to exalt his throne above God. As a result of his ambitious rebellion, he was kicked out of Heaven and exiled on earth. Satan was in the garden of Eden, when the man was formed. Like the angels, we can be sure that he was just as curious about this being that God called man. Satan, or Lucifer as he was known in Heaven was an angel who lost his position and was cursed to become a snake creeping upon the earth. He couldn't dethrone God, but this being called man was different. Obviously, the serpent spent time observing the man and listening to his conversations with God. This was a creature that could reason and speak to the man. Satan couldn't create anything to offer man, but he could pick apart what God created and plant the seeds of doubt in the mind of the man. "Did God mean what He said?" "Did God really say what you heard?" This is the same tactic the devil uses today.

Let's go back to that verse about the hostility between the seed of the serpent and the seed of the woman. God declared the outcome of that hostility. The seed of the woman would *bruise* [crush, rub out, grind] the head of the serpent, but he would only bruise his heel. Again, this was referring to Jesus Christ, and ultimately to everyone who names the Name of Jesus and bears His testimony. *"And the dragon was wroth with the woman, and went to make war with the remnant of her seed, which keep the commandments of God, and have the testimony of Jesus Christ* (Revelation 12:17)." This is why Jesus gave us power to *"tread on serpents and scorpions* (Luke 10:19)." When we walk in obedience to God and go up against the devil's kids we know that we already have the victory. Sure, they will strike at our heels, but what happens when you crush the head of the serpent? It dies.

Notice that the ones who have power over the devil are those who are obedience to God. Even Psalm 91 says that the one who can *"tread"* and *"trample,"* must be a person who *"dwells in the secret place of the Most High and abide under the shadow of the Almighty* (Psalm 91:1,13)." Jesus taught about what it means to abide. He said, *"If ye abide in me, and my words abide in you, ye shall ask what ye will, and it shall be done unto you* (John 15:7)." One who abides is one who stays under the Blessing of the Lord and does not come out to occasionally sin. It is one who trusts God with their whole heart. They know He is their only refuge from the world and the powers of darkness. They find themselves covered under *"the feathers and under his wings."* God's truth (His word) becomes their shield and buckler. It is from this position of safety in the arms of the Father that we can fight the good fight of faith against the devil. Why? When we abide in Him, all we have to do is speak the word only and the angels will fight for us. We saw how the angels went before the people of God when they went into their promised land (Exodus 23:23). The angels took out the enemies of God's people. The same is true in our day, if we speak the word of God only. As the Bible says, the angels get their commands from us, as we speak what God speaks. "Bless the LORD, ye his angels, that excel in strength, that do his commandments, hearkening unto the voice of his word. Bless ye the LORD, all [ye] his hosts; [ye] ministers of his, that do his pleasure (Psalm 103:20-21)." There you have it! We walk in power, God's power, when we obey His voice and carryout His word. In reality, it's not us, it's the Father doing the work. That is how Jesus said it. Jesus said that when you see Him, you've seen the Father. How is that possible? We said earlier that when we go in God's name, meaning that when He sends us out, we go as His agents. In the realm of the spirit, it's the same as God going Himself.

When we do what God says do, and speak what God says speak, the Father will do the work (John 14:10). Oh, He won't have to step out of Heaven to do it. The Lord has a host of angels who will do the work. They are the sent to help us carryout the will of God for our lives. Without their help, we would have no power against the devil and his angels. They will continue to war against us, not matter what we do. That was the curse that God spoke. The devil's pack will strike at our heels, but we will crush his head when we are in obedience to our Father. Our protection is a covenant promise because the battle has been set and the victory won. I recall the first time I saw this at work in my life and ministry. Back in that day, I was somewhat oblivious to the devil's actions against me. I was caught up in what God was doing. I saw the devil, but he was no concern to me. I did notice that the more victories I had for the Kingdom, the more bold the devil grew in his attacks against me. Truthfully speaking, the devil had hit me with some of his best shots before I began following the Lord wholeheartedly. God protected me when I wasn't following Him. Surely, He would protect me when I was carrying out His will. Forget that devil. I wanted to live the life God ordained for me.

Following the Lord made me the happiest I have ever been in life. That has not change to this day. I love the Lord. I love hearing and obeying His Voice. He is a good Father. I never knew what it was like to have a good father. He is a trusted friend. I had friends who turned on me when trouble came into my life. Others left when I got promoted and good things came to me. Many more left when I began following after the Lord. Even so, I am happy, and whole in my soul, and increasing more so every day. One day, the devil just couldn't take it any more. He sent people to take my life. Once that devil put a contract on my life before I began obeying God. So what, he did it again. This time, the enemy was in plain sight. The gunman was just outside of my window. The Lord told me the person was there. He said nothing more. God didn't tell me to call the police. He didn't tell me to confront the enemy. He said nothing, but I knew that if God told me, it was for me to know that He had me covered. I was secure in that knowledge alone. Later that evening, I prayed in the spirit and went to bed. Hours later, the Lord awakened me by showing how the angels were fighting the battle for me. *"Are they not all ministering spirits, sent forth to minister for them who shall be heirs of salvation* (Hebrews 1:14)?" They were jamming equipment and scrabbling tracking devices. The angels disabled the wiretaps that were placed on the phone lines. Those hulking angels were frightening to see in the spirit, yet they were working on the house and on my car supernaturally, undoing every thing the enemy set against me.

These are the types of things the angels of the Lord will do, when that devil attacks us. When we pray and obey, he cannot stop us from following God. Even as I write this book, the devil increased his death plots against my family, but God has them covered. That devil's strongest deception is that he still has power over death. Not so! Jesus took that power away from him. *"O death, where is thy sting? O grave, where is thy victory* (I Corinthians 15:55)?" After a while, the death threats from the devil become routine babble. As long as I am obeying the Lord, I have no reason to fear what the devil can do to me. So, I ignore him. I am constantly under attack, and the Lord commands me to, **"Ignore him!"** That devil is always trying to put sickness, disease, lack and death on people. When that type of attack happen, I may not know about it, but the Lord will say, **"You are exempt."** What does the scripture say? If we obey the covenant, we shall be blessed above all people . . . *"And the Lord will take away from thee all sickness, and will put none of the evil diseases of Egypt which thou knowest, upon them; but will lay them upon all them that hate thee* (Deuteronomy 7:14-15)."

Notice that God calls sickness and disease *"evil."* Of course, it's evil because it is from satan. The same is true of death. Why do you think the devil sent COVID into the world? It was to train people to fear death. That is not our portion under the Blood covenant with Jesus Christ. Do you know how many times that devil has plotted to kill me? Every attempt failed. Why? Not because of my power, but because of the power of the covenant that I have with my Father and His Son Jesus Christ. The power isn't mine. I am strong in the Lord and in the power of His might (Ephesians 6:10). Just a couple of days ago, the Lord said to me about my enemies, **"They will die in your place."** Who was God talking about? I don't know and I don't care. I have work to do. When He spoke those words, I just repeated them. "Yes, Lord they will die in my place." The "who" of the matter is not my business unless God identifies them and tells me to pray for them. Otherwise, it's just another child of the devil who is deceived enough to believe that he or she can remove God's protection and provision from my life. This is covenant. It cannot be broken. If God said, that He would curse those who cursed me, then death will be their portion if they do not repent. I pray that they do, but their outcome is God's concern, not mine. I just need to obey His word and speak what God speaks and let the Father do the work.

This is a message for today's Christian. If you can hear the voice of the Lord and obey it, the power of God will be upon you to carry out His will. Just like Jesus said, *"The spirit of the Lord is upon me, because He has anointed me* (Luke 4:18)." This is the anointing for service. When you obey the Father, that same anointing will come upon you as well. It was the anointing that empowered Jesus to cast out devils, heal the sick and raise the dead. It is available for all who believe. The Bible clearly says, *"And these signs shall follow them that believe* (Mark 16:17)." Many say they believe, but they are talking about head knowledge. Faith [real belief] requires evidence. If these signs are not following us, it is because we don't believe. I heard a word from the Lord in my spirit, years ago. I never forgot it. This word changed how I understood faith.

Here is that word. **"As kids, we played, Let's Pretend; what we will have or what we will be. But this life in Christ, we don't have to pretend. We can have what God says, if we don't faint due to pain, sickness and unbelief. If we don't receive, it's because we never really believed."**[2] This is faith in a nutshell. We have to continue to believe what God says no matter what. If we don't, then we never really had faith to begin with. Faith is certain. Faith is bold and reassured. Once you have heard from God directly, you have what is necessary to go forth in faith. After receiving this word, I never looked at the word "belief" the same again. In fact, it caused me to question others when they would say, "I'm believing God." I would respond, "What did God say about it?" I recall one minister saying, "I don't need to hear from God, I got His word in the Bible." That's not what Jesus said. When He went up against the devil in the wilderness, the enemy was quoting the Bi-

---

2   Matthews, Paula. "In Pursuit Of Super Heroic Enduring Faith." *Superheroes Of The Cross*. Los Angeles: Spirit & Life Publications, 2010. 46. Print.

ble. Jesus responded saying, *"It is written,"* however He got His words from the Father, not from the Bible. How do we know? Jesus said it Himself, *"For I have not spoken of myself; but the Father which sent me, he gave me a commandment, what I should say, and what I should speak* (John 12:49)." Jesus never said that He got the scripture from the Bible. He spoke what the Father told Him to speak, and so should we. You have to hear something from God in order to have faith. As the Bible says, *"So then faith comes by hearing . . .* (Romans 10:17)."

Perhaps you've never heard or read about Jesus in this light. Some have never been taught the truths about what it means to be a believer. The Holy Ghost was my teacher. All I did was ask and He readily taught me what I needed to know. In fact, I am ***"ever learning"*** new things about God's Kingdom, and its many mysteries to unfold. In this chapter we are unlocking the mystery about treading upon deadly things like serpents and scorpions. Shortly after my fast to break curses, the Lord gave me a *vision* that should have frightened me to no end, but it didn't. I had never seen anything like this in my whole life. *I was praying in the spirit and all of a sudden the Lord begins speaking to me about oppression that was upon me. I didn't feel anything. I didn't notice any more demonic activity than normal. Then He gave me a brief vision and all I could see were serpents all around me. They were in the airwaves so jam packed that there was no way to see through them. There was no clearing around these serpents. Then I noticed that it wasn't just me, it was the entire nation. It was as if America was overtaken by a plague of serpents. After that vision I asked the Lord what I could do. He simply said,* **"Pray more."** Let me pause here. The Lord is revealing more about this *vision*, than I saw before. The Holy Spirit is making a comparison between the *vision* and another story in the Bible.

In my spirit, I am being reminded of what happened to the Children of Israel in the wilderness. The people spoke against God, and spoke against Moses. The Lord sent *"fiery serpents"* among the people. They bit the people and many died. The people came to Moses confessing their sins and asking that he pray to God to take away the serpents. As the story goes, the Lord told Moses to make a fiery serpent out of brass and put it on a pole. It would happen that if anyone was bitten would gaze at the serpent on the pole, they would live (Numbers 21:5-9). In my vision, I saw that our nation was surrounded by snakes, whether they were fiery or not, I could not tell. All I know is that they were not biting me. In fact, the snakes around me were not even moving. I'm not even sure they were alive. Even if they were live poisonous snakes, I would be covered by God to handle any deadly thing and it not hurt me. *"They shall take up serpents; and if they drink any deadly thing, it shall not hurt them . . . (Mark 16:18)."* Not saying that we should intentionally try to pick up snakes. However, when we find ourselves in that position, we have to know that we can handle the snakes and scorpions with the help of God. The Apostle Paul took up a viper and the people who saw it, expected that he would fall dead. When that didn't happen, they thought Paul was a god (Acts 28:3-6). No! He was an ordinary man of faith who had been sent to them by God.

This brings me to question that vision: Why were the serpents there? Did God send them, or were they already there? Initially I sensed that the snakes were symbols of the deception that has infiltrated every aspect of our nation, beginning with COVID, the illegal elections, the lies about the economy, about Trump, etc. All of these things God has labeled as **"a distraction"** sent by the enemy. None of these deceptions could have succeeded had not the leaders of the Church conspired with political leaders. They have spoken against God and against His anointed remnant of believers. It's the spirit of antichrist at work in the nation and in the Church. Therefore, I prayed even **"more"** for our nation.

Then about a week or so later, the Lord gave me a *vision that was a follow-up to the one about the serpents. The Lord showed one rather large serpent that was blocking my destiny. This ugly thing was striking at anything God was sending my way. Oh, no, this devil has to go. In that vision the Lord showed me as a five year old girl, dressed in my cute dress mom made for me. I was wearing white ruffled socks with patent leather Mary Jane shoes. I took my five year old foot and smashed that big ugly serpent's head.* Listen, this wasn't a full grown Paula warring with the devil. This was a five year old kid. She didn't waiver and didn't shrink back at this huge serpent. I knew I had power to tread on that demon, no matter how big it was. All it took was one good stomp and I had conquered what the devil sent to destroy me. So, how did I do it? By obedience. In the spirit, the Lord revealed the enemy's scheme against me and told me how to disarm that thing. When I obeyed, in the spirit, I took down the enemy and left him powerless to hinder me any more. He was treaded down and trampled to the ground. This what it means that demons are *"under our feet"* in the Name of Jesus. I didn't do anything but obey in the realm of the spirit. I had no natural understanding. As I prayed in tongues, the Lord instructed to me. I repeated whatever I was told, but it was not in my understanding. Yet, it was the Lord's word in my mouth that caused deliverance to come. Once, I heard the voice of the Master, all fear was gone. In that *vision*, this five-year old had no fear. Never did it occur to me that the devil had the power to hurt me. It wasn't even a thought. I just stomped on his head and it was all over. Whatever childlike faith it took to bring me to this level in Christ, I am grateful to God. Jesus said *"Verily I say unto you, Except ye be converted, and become as little children, ye shall not enter into the kingdom of heaven. Whosoever therefore shall humble himself as this little child, the same is greatest in the kingdom of heaven* (Matthew 18:3-4)." That's it! That's the ticket. I was humble, not acting or even thinking that I knew how to take down that huge serpent. I came to Jesus as a small child in faith, knowing that the Lord had a plan that could take it down.

I am reminded of a scripture that says, *"But without faith it is impossible"* to please God. In this situation, I was definitely operating in faith. It's the second part of that scripture that caught my attention. It says, *"For he that cometh to God must believe that he is, and that he is a rewarder of them that diligently seek him* (Hebrews 11:6)." This is key. I saw the devil as a large beast. Yet, I saw my God as much bigger than the devil that was hindering me. I also knew that if God was showing me that beast, it wasn't to scare me nor to amuse me. This was something that the Lord wanted me to take down. I also believed that the Lord had the only answer that would make me victorious over the beast. If I was diligent to seek the Lord, pray and obey, that beast would be slain, and so it was.

This is how Jesus did miracles. He is our example to follow. You don't have to be some great preacher. You just have to believe what God says and do what He tells you to do. If we do the same thing Jesus did, we will get similar results. In fact, Jesus said that we would do *"greater works"* than He did (John 14:12). Here is the reason that I brought this up. People are waiting for Jesus to do for them, what Jesus empowered us to do. We have dominion in the earth. We have been given God's word. We have the Holy Spirit. This is all we need to do the wonders in the earth. It was all that Jesus had. Perhaps the only difference was the **"trust factor."** Jesus trusted the Father with His whole heart. Many of us are in the process of trusting God more and more. When we increase our **"trust factor,"** we will begin to see evidence that it's the Father in us that is doing the work. Many Christians have placed a spiritual chasm between themselves and Jesus. Yet, the Bible says, *"As he is, so are we in this world* (I John 4:17)." And, even though Jesus said that we would do the *"greater works,"* Christians have been taught that they could never do what Jesus did. They have been told that because Jesus came from God, human beings are inferior. They seem to have missed the whole point of salvation. Jesus didn't come to earth in the power of His god-ship. He came as a man, anointed by God and led by the Spirit to do good works in the earth (Acts 10:38).

That was Jesus. Think about Christians today. God is not only with us, He is in us! Therefore we have been established in righteousness. Then as the Bible says, we shall be *far from oppression*. Why? *"For thou shalt not fear: and from terror; for it shall not come near thee* (Isaiah 54:14)." Even if many devils gather together against you, like it did me that night, the Bible says that *"whosoever shall gather together against thee shall fall for thy sake* (Isaiah 54:15)." This is a covenant promise from God, but only those who believe will walk in it. Jesus came to give us back the power that was given to Adam to *"subdue"* the works of the enemy. You've got to believe the word of God and not what you see going on in the world. In the realm of the spirit, I saw serpents; nothing but serpents! Yet, I did not fear because I belong to God. I am His righteousness in Christ Jesus. I work for God and endeavor to obey Him at every turn. Therefore, whatever God shows me in the realm of the spirit is not for me to fear. It is so that I will arise in my authority and subdue whatever is hindering the work of God in the earth. I don't care if it is about me, my family, business or ministry. God has given me authority, even concerning the nation in which I live. God often shows me the position of the enemy against the Church or against the nation. Then He directs me how to pray, what to declare and decree over those circumstances.

Many people believe that Christianity is about saying a little prayer and receiving a ticket to Heaven. No! We are here to take back dominion for God's Kingdom. That requires that we become imitators of God as obedient children (Ephesians 5:1). That is what Jesus did. He came in the glory of God to show us the Father. We, as believers in Jesus Christ are to do the same. That means doing what Jesus did in this earth. Jesus gave us the same glory that He had with the Father (John 17:22). We are also commanded to make disciples of all nations. Jesus **"fixed it"** so that He did all the heavy lifting spiritually speaking. We didn't have to go to the cross. We didn't have to shed our blood, nor did we have to go to hell and take back power from the devil. Jesus did those things because it was His part of the covenant. This was what God required of Him. Jesus did all of this for us. Jesus took back from the devil everything that Adam lost. He received it for us, and then gave it all back to us. What did Jesus receive for us? Here is what the Bible reveals. *"And I beheld, and I heard the voice of many angels round about the throne and the beasts and the elders: and the number of them was ten thousand times ten thousand, and thousands of thousands; Saying with a loud voice, Worthy is the Lamb that was slain to receive power, and riches, and wisdom, and strength, and honour, and glory, and blessing* (Revelation 5:11-12)."

Consider this. Jesus was Blessed in Heaven with the Father, where He possessed power and riches and wisdom and strength and honor and glory and blessing. Jesus already had these things in Heaven. Yet, He willingly left the richest life in Heaven to care about us here on earth. The Apostle Paul said, *"Let this mind be in you, which was also in Christ Jesus."* *"Who, being in the form of God, thought it not robbery to be equal with God: but made himself of no reputation, and took upon him the form of a servant, and was made in the likeness of men: and being found in fashion as a man, he humbled himself, and became obedient unto death, even the death of the cross* (Philippians 2:5-8)." Jesus *humbled* Himself and chose to come to earth in the form of a man. Are you hearing this? God left Heaven and came to earth. You remember what the angel told the Virgin Mary. *"Also that holy thing which shall be born of thee shall be called the Son of God* (Luke 1:35)." *"And they shall call His Name Emmanuel, which being interpreted is, God with us* (Matthew 1:23)."

Jesus, who is God, left Heaven and humbled Himself in the form of a man, but not just any man. Jesus was obedient to God, even when it hurt. Jesus was tempted like we are, but without sin (Hebrews 4:15). Still, God made Him to be sin for our sakes. Jesus agreed to take on the curse on that cross, just so that He could die, go to hell and take the keys of hell and death back from the devil (Revelation 1:18). Jesus resurrected from the grave saying, *"All power is given unto me in heaven and in earth* (Matthew 28:18)." Then Jesus turns to us, the Church saying, *"Go Ye"* in my name, with My power and change the world! Jesus gave us power to change every evil situation in the earth. He's not coming back until our part is done. I know that is a surprise to some Christians because they have been taught that Jesus is coming back to finish what He started! No! Jesus did it all! As He said on the cross *"It is finished* (John 19:30)." His part on earth is finished. Next time Jesus shows up He is coming as the reigning King of God's Kingdom. He is coming in the power of His Father to set up His earthly throne. In the meantime, Jesus gave us back the power that Adam forfeited in the garden. Jesus gave us back the riches and wisdom, the strength, honor and glory and blessing that Adam lost. Jesus also gave us back the keys of hell and death. I will never forget the *visions* the Lord gave me concerning hell. *I was praying in tongues and all of a sudden I found myself standing in hell with Jesus. The Lord was teaching me something about our authority over death and hell.* Then I recall the time I was watching Gloria Copeland's Healing School online. That previous evening while sleeping, the fire of God came on me. I asked the Lord what was going on. He said, **"The word is healing you."** The word I had heard preached earlier that day was working on me during my sleep. So, I received my complete healing and went back to sleep. The next morning again, while listening to scriptures on healing, I had a *vision. I was walking in hell. I saw the torment of death. The Lord was with me although I didn't see Him. He placed something in my hands. It was very big, like a large case of keys to hell and death.* What this meant, I did not know.

Now, I'm going to be very transparent about what I have learned about hell. Demons are **"critters"** from hell. They do the bidding of satan in order to put people in bondage. Around the same time that I had the first *vision* of hell, *the Lord gave me another vision in which I was being released from an underground pit. I was taken from the deepest level in the earth, through what seemed like an ocean of water. When I came up out of the water, my brother was standing there with his hands extended to pull me out. He looked like a giant superhero. When I came out of that ocean, I was immediately transformed into an even bigger superhero.* It reminded me of what the Lord told me when I first accepted my assignment in Cleveland, Ohio. The Lord quoted Psalm 16:10, "For thou wilt not leave my soul in hell; neither wilt thou suffer thine Holy One to see corruption."

Some of you might be wondering how I came to be in hell and in bondage so many times. First of all, it was my assignment. It came about in a most unusual manner. I was agitated at the devil for interfering in my promises. God would make a promise and the devil would either scare people away, or have someone steal what was rightfully mine. I didn't understand why this kept happening because the Lord made a strong promise to me. He said that He **"would cause men to give to me."** It came from a demonstration that occurred during a church service. What I experienced instead were men stealing from me. Powerful men, leaders in the Church and in the government prayed evil prayers over me just to keep me from getting what God said was mine. God called them *"fornicators."* They all had a hatred for me and for what I stood for. Consequently, they hired witches to set traps for me. They came from the highest level of the occult trying to stop me. Instead of men who would give to me, these were *"marauders and robbers"* who the devil sent in an attempt to stop me. I was even accosted on the streets of Los Angeles by a man who said that he and his friends paid "good money" for me. They claimed to "own me." I should have called the police and had him arrested, but I was so appalled that I blasted the man with the word of God. I let Him know that God owned me; that I was bought with the precious Blood of Jesus. That devil ran away from me. Why? I had power over all the power of the enemy. Nothing shall by any means hurt me. Yet, that does not stop the devil from trying. That's all he knows to do. At least he's consistent. If every Christian would be just as consistent to do good as that devil and his lot does evil, this thing could wrap up in no time flat and Jesus would come take us out of here! But, it's God's plan, not mine. He knew we'd be in our present state. God alone knows how to catapult us into His divine will. And, He will do it, in His time, in Jesus' Name!

Here is the point. After those encounters with hell, I would never tell someone to go to hell. I would never wish that on any human being. Hell was never created for us. It was created for the devil and his angels (Matthew 25:41). No human being should ever desire to go to that horrid place of eternal torment. Yet, people end up there. Here is the reason why. They reject Jesus. It's not because they are gay. Stop! For all you Christians who have been told that all gay people go to hell, repent. The Bible never said that. What sends a person to hell is the rejection of Jesus Christ and His sacrifice for our sins. If we reject Jesus, then we pay for our own sins. That's what sends people to hell. Here is a news flash! There are some in the Church calling themselves Christians who may very well find themselves in the Lake of Fire. Revelation 21:8 is addressed to the Church of Jesus Christ. *"But the fearful, and unbelieving, and the abominable, and murderers, and whoremongers, and sorcerers, and idolaters, and all liars, shall have their part in the lake which burneth with fire and brimstone: which is the second death."* Look at the order! First up is *the fearful*! The Lord is talking about cowards in the Church. Stop right there. We don't have to go any further.

So many believers live in fear, which opens the portal for the devil to rule in their lives. Fear is the devil's greatest tactic against the Church of Jesus Christ. The Lord gave me a word in the middle of the night saying, **"The root [cause] of all evil is the love of money, but the portal of ALL EVIL is FEAR."** Then in my spirit I heard this scripture, *"For where envying and strife [is], there [is] confusion and every evil work* (Jame 3:16)." Think about why people envy others? Why do they cause strife? One word. FEAR.

We are in an age in which the devil has been plaguing mankind with schemes that invoke fear. As a result, people are warring with one another out of fear; the fear of losing freedom, fear of losing their lives and livelihood. This is not God's purpose for our lives. Fear is a spirit. It's demonic. It comes from the serpent, not from God. *"For God hath not given us the spirit of fear; but of power, and of love, and of a sound mind* (II Timothy 1:7)." No matter how ugly this world gets, we cannot afford to fear. As believers in Jesus Christ, we have been given power. We have the love of God in us. Therefore if we know that God loves us, then we will also know He will take care of us. We who are saved, also have the Holy Ghost, who is also called the Mind of Christ. Therefore, no believer should fall prey to fear. We have been armed against that spirit. Fear empowers that devil. Remember it's a portal; a door. But, hold on. There is good news! The love of God opens the portal to Every Good Thing! Love empowers the Spirit of God. Seek God. Seek His Love and everything you need will flow into your lives. **"Be Intentional"** to turn from evil and do good. It's a choice as simple as turning a faucet from hot to cold water. When you make that turn you will go from fear to love, from lack to abundance, from the curse into the Blessing of the Lord.

We've been talking about serpents and scorpions, which may sound ominous, but they are a spiritual reality. Which is why we need to **"Be Intentional,"** to do things God's way. *"Trust in the LORD with all thine heart; and lean not unto thine own understanding. In all thy ways acknowledge him, and he shall direct thy paths* (Proverbs 3:5-6)." Pray about everything. Give every thing to God. We are called to The Blessing, that door is always open to us. But again, one must **"Be intentional"** to choose (Deuteronomy 30:19). We've talked about the law of seedtime and harvest. It holds true for our offspring, for they are our seed. We must **"Be intentional"** about how we cultivate our seed to bring forth a godly harvest with fruit that remains. Here is a *"corollary"* to that law. You also came from a seed. Whose seed are you? Someone in authority over your life may have made decisions that caused a curse to come upon you, your family, a people or a nation. It can result in death, financial losses, plagues [pandemics], famine [droughts and food shortages]. That is where we are in the world today. Those in authority have done such evil in the sight of God. Now, the families of the earth are suffering. That is why we see war all around us. It's not the people. It's the leaders who brought forth the evil. This is also why the Lord called me to a fast. We may not be able to break the curses off all nations. Our authority cannot override the will of others. However, Jesus gave us power to break curses over our own lives and over that of our families. This goes back to the GENERATIONAL BLESSING that was upon the life of Abraham. Jesus broke the spiritual barrier that promoted the generational curse. That is why I was able to fast and pray to break the curses off of my family. It's up to each of you to take authority over your own lives, through Christ. ***"Be Intentional."*** Tell God what you want out of this life and let Him tell you His plan. You will hear of wars and rumors of wars. DO NOT FEAR! God has the solution for each of us. You need only to ask Him.

The Lord also warns us to ***"Pay attention to your dreams. They are spiritual."*** Evil serpents roam at night while people are sleeping. Beware of sexual encounters while you sleep. Someone may try to put a ring on your finger or get you to sign a contract in your sleep. He may try to get you to ingest something. If it happens. Shut it down! If you can not react fast enough then just repent and renounce any covenant or vow that was entered without your full knowledge and consent. The devil attacks at night to catch us at a weak moment. God has given you a way to get back at that slithering creep. And, whatever your need or desire, whether for a spouse, or a position or for any particular thing, take it to God in prayer.

The Bible says that God will supply *"all your need"* according to His riches in glory by Christ Jesus (Philippians 4:19). Let the Lord lead your life, and you will not lack anything you need or desire (Psalm 23:1). Also, let God supply whatever you need, not according to your standards, but according to His. Did you know that God can get anything to you from anywhere in the earth? You do know, that the earth and everything in it belongs to God (Psalm 24:1). You, oh believer also belong to God. He is a good Father who will make sure His kids have an abundance of every good thing Heaven and earth have to offer. Plus, God has ***"unlimited possibilities"*** awaiting each of us. God was intentional when He created mankind in His image and His likeness. God was intentional when He put Jesus on that cross to redeem us back from hell. The Heavenly Father was very, intentional when He raised Jesus from the dead saying, *"Thy throne, O God, [is] for ever and ever: a sceptre of righteousness [is] the sceptre of thy kingdom* (Hebrews 1:8)." Likewise, the Father was intentional when He called us out of darkness into His marvelous Light. God was intentional when He imparted to us His DNA, making us His workmanship in Christ preordained to do good works. The Father was also intentional when He sent Jesus to demonstrate how to walk as Kingdom sons and daughters in this earth. God was intentional when He gave us the Holy Spirit to teach and guide us to His perfect will for our lives. So, let us too, **"Be intentional"** about walking in love, not fear, and trusting the Father for whatever we need. He truly a good Father who loves us and has many good things for His kids.

> *"He that overcometh shall inherit all things;*
> *And I will be his God, and he shall be my son."*
> Revelation 21:7

Tearing Down Familial Altars

Throughout this book, we have mentioned altars, which play a crucial role in the realm of the spirit. An altar is a place of worship, prayer and sacrifice, most often to a deity or god. However, some people make altars of worship to other people, ideologies or human achievements. Such altars can be in the form of photographs, ritual tables, even edifices of all sorts. In an earlier chapter, we mentioned the Tower of Babel. That was an edifice built by men to honor themselves instead of worshiping and honoring God. Let's be honest. God created us to worship. Therefore, if mankind does not worship the Almighty God, they will find someone or some thing else to worship. It's in our nature to do so. Here's what is important to note about altars. They serve as a *portal*, or a door to the world of the supernatural. It was God who created altars for His own purposes. It is the place where He made covenants with mankind.

Long before there were temples of worship, Noah built an altar to the Lord. So did, Abraham and Moses. Altars became the place where mortal men were able to communicate with a holy God. It was a bridge to the world of the supernatural. When we talk about the supernatural world, we are talking about the multidimensional plane which surrounds the planet. It includes what we would call both the heavens [atmosphere] just above the earth, and the vast expanse of space that lies between earth's atmosphere and Heaven where God resides.

For our purposes, when we mention the supernatural we are referring to beings and activity that exist under what the Bible calls *"the third heaven."* The Apostle Paul talked about being *"caught up to the third heaven."* He was *"caught up into paradise, and heard unspeakable words, which it is not lawful for a man to utter* (II Corinthians 12:4)." It was in this *"third heaven"* that Paul received *"visions and revelations of the Lord."* He never spoke about an altar, nor what he was doing that put him in the position to be caught up. Yet, it remains important to note that this man received supernatural mysteries when he made contact with the holy God in Heaven. It also stands to reason that if there is a third heaven, there must also be a first and a second heaven. There is the heaven we see existing above the earth. That is where we see the clouds, the sun and that sign of God's covenant, the rainbow.

This is considered the first heaven. Evidence of the second heaven is in the story of Daniel who fasted and prayed for his nation. The response from God was held up by a battle between God's angels and the demons prince angels in the heavens (Daniel 10:7-14). There was no battle in the earth. The battle occurred in the heavens between the third heaven where God resides and the second heaven. That is the realm where both God's angels and the dark angels do battle over the people and situations of the earth. The angels of the Lord **"traverse"** between the third Heaven and earth, amid the warfare with satan's dark angels.

What's fascinating about Daniel's story is that the angel told him exactly how and when God answered his prayer. *"Then said he unto me, Fear not, Daniel: for from the first day that thou didst set thine heart to understand, and to chasten thyself before thy God, thy words were heard, and I am come for thy words* (Daniel 10:12)." In this passage, we learn that Daniel made contact with God through prayer *"from the first day."* This should help somebody reading this. Daniel was able to get an immediate answer to his prayers. Unfortunately, the answer was held up getting to him, but nonetheless God answered on the same day the man prayed. Let's explore how he got his prayer through so quickly.

The Bible says that Daniel prayed on his knees before the Lord three times a day (Daniel 6:10). It's not clear whether he had a physical altar, but he definitely made contact with God because he had an **"altar of the heart."** This is key to understand about prayer. It's not just talking to God with many words. It's communicating from your heart to God. We speak and we listen. Often we tend to pray everything that's on our mind and stop praying. We hang up on God before He has a chance to answer. That's not prayer. That's one-sided conversation. Prayer is worship. It's a time to honor God and love on Him and then give Him our request. It's a time to see what's on His heart. What does God need from us, not so much what He can do for us. Enough said. Let's move on. We're talking about altars.

One does not need to build an altar made of stone or wood to interact with God. You don't even need to pray on your knees like Daniel did. God desires a certain **"heart posture"** from us. Jesus said it this way, " . . . *the hour cometh, when ye shall neither in this mountain, nor yet at Jerusalem, worship the Father . . . But the hour cometh, and now is, when the true worshippers shall worship the Father in spirit and in truth: for the Father seeketh such to* *worship him. God [is] a Spirit: and they that worship him must worship [him] in spirit and in truth (John 4:21-24)."* God is looking for those who have a heart to worship Him in spirit and in truth. This is how to get answered prayer. *"For the eyes of the LORD run to and fro throughout the whole earth, to shew himself strong in the behalf of them whose heart is perfect toward him (II Chronicles 16:9)."* This also how Daniel prayed. He *"set"* his heart to receive wisdom and understanding from the Lord. He also **"humbled"** himself before God. That's what it means to *"chasten"* one's self. In other words, Daniel diligently sought to reach the God of Heaven (Hebrews 11:6). In doing so, he built an *"altar of the heart"* and God responded immediately by sending a messenger angel to him. The angel told Daniel that his **"words were heard."** The angel came for Daniel's words. We also mentioned this in the previous chapter. The angels of the Lord respond when we speak (voice) the word of God. Angels also come for our words, to execute what God has put into our mouth to speak (Psalm 103:20). This is why even in prayer, we should *"speak the word only (Matthew 8:8)."* New covenant saints should not only have an *"altar of the heart,"* but should know that our bodies are *"the temple"* of the Holy Spirit (I Corinthians 6:19). It was not so in the old covenant. This is unique to the new creature in Christ. Since Christ is in us (Colossians 1:27), we don't reach up to Heaven to hear from God. He's in us. The Kingdom is within us. Therefore, the answers we are seeking, are within us. Our prayers don't have to go up to Heaven. We must release them from within us. Our bodies are *"the temple"* but the altar is our heart, which includes our soul (mind, will, emotions, intellect). Sometimes the answers we need are blocked because of unbelief, or doubt. If the heart is the door, then is must align itself with the spirit in order to release the answers we need in this life. Remember that the Kingdom, God's entire Kingdom is within us. The altar of our hearts must align itself with the spirit making us *"one"* in worship and prayer. This is the spiritual atmosphere of agreement that causes prayers to be answered *"from the first day"* like it was with Daniel. Again, we are the temple and our hearts are **"re-created"** and **"calibrated"** to receive the things of God. Therefore, we must guard our hearts and flow with God. We must also honor the Lord and glorify Him in our bodies which belong to Him.

Now, if anyone earnestly goes after (builds an altar to) a demon god or evil power dark angels will also come for his or her words. God gave mankind dominion over the earth. No spirit can enter the realm of the earth without our permission. Almighty God can't even enter the earth without human permission. *"The heaven, [even] the heavens, [are] the LORD'S: but the earth hath he given to the children of men* (Psalm 115:16)." Please understand what this means. If demonic forces are active in your home, it is because someone invited them in. If demons are taking over your city, state or nation, it is also because someone opened the portal to let them in. God has very strong words for those to build altars to other deities, yet people do it all the time. Whether it is summoning up the spirits of their elders, or bringing people from the dead, these practices are against the law of God and they bring curses upon people's lives.

Many curses are tied to our ethnic cultures, traditions and beliefs. Things that people refuse to get rid of because their ancestors did the same thing for centuries. I remember when God called me into ministry. I had to renounce the practices of my family in witchcraft, soothsaying, healing arts from both African and Native American traditions. These things were in my spirit. They were familiar to me, even though no one taught me. I never knew these ancestors. Even so, the Lord had me renounce **"the spiritual mixtures that had polluted my spirit."** I did so my renouncing the rituals and traditions of my ancestors that prevented the Blessing of the Lord from manifesting in my life. God had me *"confess"* with my mouth, **"the sole lordship"** of Jesus Christ over my life (Romans 10:9). I was already saved. Jesus was my Lord. That is how I answered the call to ministry, but I was not yet **"purified"** for service. "*And he shall sit as a refiner and purifier of silver: and he shall purify the sons of Levi, and purge them as gold and silver, that they may offer unto the LORD an offering in righteousness* (Malachi 3:3)." I was sanctified. Which means that I was saved and set aside for God's holy purpose, but I was in no way **"prepared and equipped"** to step out into ministry, in the arena where the devil was looking for prey. God said He was doing **"a quick work"** in me, and indeed He did that.

We're talking about tearing down familiar or family altars. Some people don't understand the purpose in doing so. The Lord gave me the perfect example to use. Years ago, I went to the home of a close friend of mine. She offered me something to drink. As we stepped into her dimly lit kitchen, she reached into the dishwasher and brought out a glass. From my vantage point, I saw a bold lipstick print on the rim of the glass. When I told her the glass was dirty, she replied, "It's not dirty. I just took it out of the dishwasher." Even so, I let her know that I could see the dirt on the glass. My friend became offended and began to pour a liquid in the glass. Rather than argue with her, I flipped on the overhead lights in the kitchen. It was only then that she saw just how dirty that glass was. Not only was there a lipstick stain on the rim, but there was also sediment at the bottom of the glass. God has used this example so many times to describe His people. They think because they get saved, that they are cleaned up and ready to receive all that Heaven has for us. No! Salvation is just the beginning. There are many levels of transition and deliverance needed.

One would never join the US Armed Services and expect to immediately walk in the power and benefits of the military. You have to make it through Boot Camp first. You have to endure the pain of sacrificing your body and mind for the sake of service. The same is true in God's Kingdom. *"What? Know ye not that your body is the temple of the Holy Ghost [which is] in you, which ye have of God, and ye are not your own? For ye are bought with a price: therefore glorify God in your body, and in your spirit, which are God's* (I Corinthians 6:19-20)." Oh, Christian, sacrifices must be made. Your mind must be renewed (Romans 12:1-2). You are no longer your own. You belong to Christ. You have enlisted in the Army of God. Give no place to your enemy, the devil.

We are talking about altars. So who started the process of using altars in the first place? According to the Bible, altars were introduced and established by Almighty God. After Adam sinned, mankind could no longer commune with God face-to-face. Sin had separated us. Yet God wanted to restore communication with mankind. For that to happen, He couldn't leave us in our sin. God established a **"covenant precedent"** by slaying an animal and covering the man and his wife with the coats of skins (Genesis 3:21). The Bible gives us no details about an altar of sacrifice in this case, however we can figure that at least one animal had to give up its life to cover the sinful man and his wife. Which brings us to the actual **"covenant precedent"** that God and His Son Jesus established before the worlds began. The Bible calls Jesus *"the Lamb of God, which taketh away the sin of the world* (John 1:29). The Bible also lets us know that Jesus, the Lamb of God was slain *"from the foundation of the world* (Revelation 13:8)." Therefore, from scripture we understand that animal sacrifices were deemed necessary offerings for sin. God and Jesus established such before creation on earth began. In other words, God had a plan to deal with our sins even before mankind was created. When God clothed the man and his wife in skins, we can also assume that the sacrifice was made in their presence. Who built an altar, God or man? Who killed the animal (s) and took the skins, God or man? Regardless of who did what in this sacrifice, God set the pattern for a *"familial altar"* for a sin offering. Man had to be given a demonstration of what it meant for flesh to die, along with an explanation as to why a sin offering was necessary. How do we know? Later in the Bible we read how Cain and Abel, the sons of Adam, were presenting sacrifices before God. *"And the Lord had respect unto Abel and to his offering: But unto Cain and to his offering he had not respect* (Genesis 4:3-5)." Who taught them about offerings and sacrifices? Obviously, God taught Adam and the man taught his sons.

We find out later in the life of Noah, that God commanded that a life be given for that which was taken. *"Whoso sheddedth man's blood, by man shall his blood be shed: for in the image of God made he man* (Genesis 9:4-6)." It is interesting to note that this was not required when Cain killed Abel. God put a mark on Cain forbidding anyone to take his life. Instead he was sent *"cursed from the earth"* to live as a *"fugitive and a vagabond* (Genesis 4:10-15)." In the garden, the process of death had begun. The man and his wife were clothed with glory no more. Their sin and their nakedness was exposed. The fig leaves covered their nakedness, but only shed blood would cover their sin. The curse of death that Adam put into motion, had now taken the life of his son Abel. The blood of Abel spoke as a witness against his brother. God in Heaven heard it. *"And he said, What hast thou done? The voice of thy brother's blood crieth unto me from the ground* (Genesis 4:10)." Notice how Adam's generations began operating in the curse of death. God instituted the altar and sacrifice to redeem man from the penalty of death. This is how mankind was suppose to give worship and homage to the Creator God, in order to stay within His Blessing. However, mankind would later use the *"altar concept"* to turn away from God to worship idols. This is where we are today. People are snared in curses because of the generations who built altars to false gods. These evil altars must be torn down before the Blessing of the Lord can manifest fully in one's life.

Remember how we said that we don't have to build an altar, but that it is the *"altar of the heart"* that connects with the supernatural world, either for good or for evil. Years ago, my church went on a fast. Friends and I decided to pray and connect with one another daily as we went through the fast. Well, one particular friend didn't want to connect. She fasted with anger and resentment. When the fast was over, most of us saw the Hand of God moving miraculously in our lives. However, this one person had invited demonic forces to come into her life. This period of fasting was supposed to be for us to *"afflict our soul* (Isaiah 58:3)*"* so that our voices could be heard by God. It is required that the flesh (the soul, will, imagination, emotions, intellect) be brought under subjection to the born again spirit. During the fast our friend did not yield herself to the Lord. Instead, she let her flesh marinate in anger causing demonic forces to overtake her. Because the altar of her heart was wicked, that woman conjured up demons spirits instead.

Jesus talked about the **"altar of the heart"** in another way. *"A good man out of the good treasure of the heart bringeth forth good things: and an evil man out of the evil treasure bringeth forth evil things* (Matthew 12:35).*"* Human beings are prone to blame others for what comes into their lives, but Jesus tells us the truth about the matter. It's the law of seedtime and harvest. We reap what we sow. No one does it to us. We do it to ourselves. *"For from within, out of the heart of men, proceed evil thoughts, adulteries, fornications, murders, thefts, covetousness, wickedness, deceit, lasciviousness, an evil eye, blasphemy, pride, foolishness: All these evil things come from within, and defile the man* (Mark 7:21-23).*"* If evil is happening to us, we must make sure it's not coming through us because of the evil **"altar of the heart."** Many of us are snared because of what's in our hearts. Sometimes we take on the attitudes of those around us, unknowingly.

Something evil happened to me recently and the reaction that came out of my human spirit shocked me. I heard words that I had never thought before, but they were inside of my heart. Immediately I repented and asked the Holy Spirit to remove those words from inside of me. Fortunately the words never came out of my mouth. I heard them come out of my soul and immediately cast them out. When the Bible tells us to diligently guard our hearts, it's for a good reason.*"Keep thy heart with all diligence; for out of it [are] the issues of life* (Proverbs 4:23).*"* The enemy is always shooting his fiery darts to ignite evil thoughts in our hearts. This is when we need that part of our spiritual armor called the *"shield of faith* (Ephesians 6:16).*"* We know what the Bible says. We know how we should be responding to things around us. Every once and a while, some thing comes up inside us causing us to say, "That's not me. Where did that come from?" Root it up. Don't pretend that you didn't hear it. The Holy Spirit is bringing that tree to your attention. As Jesus said, *"Every plant, which my heavenly Father hath not planted, shall be rooted up* (Matthew 15:13).*"* Sometimes these are trees, or ways of thinking that come from our parents, our traditions or culture. If it is not a thought that is consistent with what God says, it has to be *"rooted up," if you want the Blessing of the Lord to fully manifest in your lives. Let's for a moment talk about how culture shapes the *"altar of the heart."* In America, we have a culture that hates God. Unfortunately, many Christians agree with the culture because they identify with being an American more than being a citizen of God's Kingdom. This is a *"familial altar"* that must come down. Coming from the African American culture, I see the same thing. Some people stand on the principle that they are Black in a racist culture rather than seeing themselves as citizens of a Kingdom that cannot be shaken. If you are a Black person in America, you are expected to live a certain way. You are expected to believe a certain way. In fact, one who sits in the White House as I write, even went as far as telling us that African American voters are very predictable. That sounds like another *"familial altar"* to me. However Jesus said something about the believer that should be noted. He said that because we are spiritual beings, we are like the wind. *"The wind bloweth where it listeth, and thou hearest the sound thereof, but canst not tell whence it cometh, and whither it goeth: so is every one that is born of the Spirit* (John 3:8)." In other words, *"unpredictability is the hallmark of the spirit led believer."*

What saith God to all of us who have built altars to idols; of entertainers, or politicians, or ideas or money or material things, or anything thing created. God said, *"Thou shalt have no other gods before me* (Exodus 20:3)." So, why do we do it? It goes back to why people make covenants. They believe that the idol can give them something they don't naturally possess. Or they believe, like our early example of the woman who wanted a man, that the only way to get him was to go to an herbalist to get a charm. Idolatry is a major issue in the Body of Christ. It's not only about serving other gods. It's about worshiping other people and things more than we worship the Creator God. We tend to build altars to our money, and our possessions. They become things of worship. Some people build altars to other people, which is a bit creepy. These people tend to be crazed maniacs and stalkers. Yet, they use evil demon powers to seek after other people. We call them idol worshipers, but they are criminals. In any case, here is the issue. People are suffering. They are hurting and confused as the issues of the world escalate. Some are calling on God. That's a good thing. However, many are asking why God left us. Really? He never left us. We left Him. In response to this question, the Lord took me to the story of Gideon (Judges 6), which represents what many people are experiencing in our day. The Children of Israel did evil in the sight of the Lord. They were delivered into the hands of their enemies for seven years. The enemy prevailed so much against them that God's people hid in dens and caves in fear. Whatever the people planted for food, the Midianites would come up against them and destroy the increase of their fields. The enemy also destroyed their cattle. *"Israel was greatly impoverished because of the Midianites; and the children of Israel cried unto the Lord* (Judges 6:6)." Let's take America for example. We have done much evil in the sight of the Lord. Consequently, we have tyrants over our nation who are imposing wicked restrictions upon the people. The enemy is doing all in his power to impoverish the people and terrorize them with fear; even to the point creating of shortages and destroying the increase of our fields with a lack of workers. No matter what the enemy is doing through our leadership, it happened because the people, God's people specifically, did evil in the sight of the Lord.

When the attack grew severe enough, Gideon and the Children of Israel cried out to God in prayer. In America, prayer wasn't our first resort. It was our last resort when all other measures failed. What happened to us? Why did we fall into evil? The Book of Judges explains how the Children of Israel had historically witnessed divine miracles. However, there would come a period in which the people forgot their God and turned to idols. *"And also all that generation were gathered unto their fathers: and there arose another generation after them, which knew not the LORD, nor yet the works which he had done for Israel. And the children of Israel did evil in the sight of the LORD, and served Baalim: And they forsook the LORD God of their fathers, which brought them out of the land of Egypt, and followed other gods, of the gods of the people that [were] round about them, and bowed themselves unto them, and provoked the LORD to anger. And . . . served Baal and Ashtaroth. And the anger of the LORD was hot against Israel, and he delivered them into the hands of spoilers that spoiled them . . . so that they could not any longer stand before their enemies. . . . Nevertheless the LORD raised up judges, which delivered them out of the hand of those that spoiled them*(Judges 2:10-16)."

From this back drop, the story of Gideon begins. Today, our story is quite the same. We've heard of previous generations who saw miraculous works of God. Many old timers speaks of divine encounters as if they were a thing of the past. Consequently, the younger generations never received the faith to expect miracles in their lifetime. We are currently living in a generation, even a generation of Christians who don't know the miraculous power and provision of God. I even recall a conversation with a Baptist preacher who was teaching that we don't need the Holy Spirit and the supernatural gifts of God any more. Why? He said that we had technology instead. Unfortunately this is what many people believe. Therefore, we are a people who have forgotten the God of our fathers. The Bible records how the people of God in Bible days would turn away from God and find themselves oppressed by their enemies. Then they would cry out to God for salvation. That is what we are seeing today. For the first time in decades, Christians and heathen alike are praying for God to save them from what is going on in their nations. The people of the world are yearning to be free from tyrannical leaders. They have been oppressed by sickness, disease, food shortages, financial hardships, which has brought about fear and wars. Clearly we have fallen into the hands of the evil one, for a season. In America, the Lord said that we were *"in strong delusion."* Because we didn't have a love for the truth, God sent a *"strong delusion"* that we would receive a lie. Our trust was in men rather than in God. Therefore we fell into the schemes of the evil one. Think about what happened with Gideon. These were God's people who did evil in the sight of the Lord. After being oppressed by the devil, Gideon asked the angel of the Lord, *"Oh, my Lord, if the Lord be with us, why then is all this befallen us? And where be all his miracles which our fathers told us of, saying Did not the Lord bring us up from Egypt? But now the Lord hath forsaken us, and delivered us into the hands of the Midianites* (Judges 6:13)."

Many believers have felt like they were forsaken by the Lord. But, we have a promise from God. *"For he hath said, I will never leave thee, nor forsake thee* (Hebrews 13:5)." God even said that there are unbelievers who have heard about His wonders. They are asking "Where is the god of the Bible?" This is a dangerous question to ask. When Gideon ask about the miracles of his fathers, the Lord said to him, *"Go in this thy might and thou shalt save Israel* (Judges 6:14)." When one asks this type of question of God, it is a set up for God to do the miraculous through you. This type of question demonstrates that one has a hope that the God of wonders would show up in their situation. They have heard of such a God and are diligently searching to find out if what was said about Him is true. This is the kind of person God is looking for. They may not have strong faith that He exists, but they are willing to seek the truth about God. When we seek answers about God's power, He often responds by demonstrating that power through us.

We are still talking about tearing down *"familial altars"* of our culture, nation or family. Gideon's story is the example we are following. The answer we seek begins with us. All God needed to free Israel was one man. That man was Gideon. Therefore, all God needs to free your family, your city, even your nation, is one person. That person could be you. Don't look to mankind for your nation's solution. It's not there. Look to God and He will show you the specific solution for your circumstance. It doesn't matter to God who you are or where you came from. He just needs *"a willing heart."* Remember that God can work through the *"altar of the heart."* Indeed, God is looking for a willing heart. On the other hand, the devil is also looking for *"a willing heart"* for prey. *"Be sober, be vigilant; because your adversary the devil, as a roaring lion, walketh about, seeking whom he may devour* (I Peter 5:8)." This is why we must guard our hearts and be diligent to follow after God. He can take the least among us and make him or her the greatest. In fact, that's promise He made to Abraham. That is exactly what God did with Gideon. That is why his story is in the Bible and why we are studying him today.

Gideon was introduced to the God of his forefathers. Although he was part of a generation estranged from God, Gideon soon learned to trust and have confidence in God. As a result, he built an altar to the Lord calling it *"Jehovashalom,"* the Lord is peace (Judges 6:24). That same night the Lord told Gideon to take his father's bullock and *"throw down"* the altar of Baal that his father had built and *"cut down"* the grove by it (Judges 6:25-26). God told him to take the bullock and build an altar to the Lord in that place even with the wood of the grove that had been cut. Before God would sent Gideon out to battle against the Midianites, he had to *"thrown down"* the altar his father built and build an altar to the Lord in its place. Herein is **"the crux"** of the message. **"Before we can take out our enemies, we must remove the enemy from our own camp."** God is very specific in His maneuvers. If we ask Him to take out the trash from our lives, we must make sure we are not still holding on to trash. The word of God is sharper than any two-edged sword (Hebrews 4:12). It's sure to cut both ways. If you ask God to remove the enemy, He will do a **"clean sweep"** of anything labeled "enemy." Make sure there is no enemy in you. That is why God could send Gideon against the enemy, to first destroy the altar of Baal that his father built. Gideon knew that the men of the city would be after him because they had all sold out to worship Baal. So, Gideon ventured out at night and tore down the altar. The next morning the men of the city found out who tore down the altar and came after Gideon to take his life. These were the generations, who like Gideon's father, had turned from the Lord to serve idols. This was the evil in the sight of God that led them captive to their enemies. Let me stop here to address something that has happened in the United States.

God has been talking to me about a *"lost generation,"* in the Church. These are elders who turned away from God to follow after religion, culture and politics. They put their trust in man, leaving behind a *"fatherless generation"* in this world of darkness. We yearn for spiritual parents to show us the way back to the God of miracles, yet they have forgotten the way. According to the Lord, *"they taught us to honor men instead of honoring God."* Today, America is under satanic rule because the people chose to honor men of longevity instead of men of righteousness. The Church was blind. They failed to notice that it was during the past sixty-years of leadership that prayer was taken out of school, abortion was legalized, and the ten commandments were outlawed in public buildings. The Church did nothing. God revealed that this was the same generation who received their social mores from television. The world influenced the Church with its vision, and darkness was allowed to prevail. It therefore should be no surprise that after the 2020 presidential election a demon appeared in the realm of the spirit, declaring that America belonged to it. Who was this demonic presence? We have a covenant with God. How could a demon claim America? Almighty God said that the election was not so much about who was in the White House. It was about *"Whom America will serve."*[1]

The Lord has given me great hope that *"America shall be saved."* Then something wondrous happened. The people began praying earnestly and God heard their cries. Like Gideon, a new generation has been crying out for the God of miracles. I saw God responding by removing the altar of Baal from over this land. It was Almighty God who by His power overturned the Supreme Court decision of Roe versus Wade. Sure, it was the vote of men and women on the court. However, when the people prayed earnestly, it made much power from God available. His Spirit pierced the hearts of those on the courts. As the Bible says, *"The effectual fervent prayer of a righteous man availeth much* (James 5:16).*"* Some might be wondering what this has to do with the altar to Baal. Part of Baal worship is the sacrifice of children. The demon Moloch also requires the blood of chil-

---

[1] Matthews, Paula. "Waging A Warfare." *Taking Back The Night.* Atlanta: Spirit & Life Publications℠, 2020. 120. Print.

dren in its rituals. When a woman has an abortion, it may seem like she is exercising her right to choose what to do with her body. Yet, in the spirit that woman is actually making a choice to sacrifice her unborn child to the demon gods. I understand how hard this is to believe. I have heard testimony from women who have had abortions and were told that to be totally free they had to renounce the covenant they made with the demon Moloch. These women had unknowingly sacrificed their babies to an idol. When the women renounced their covenant with Moloch, they were totally healed, spirit, soul and body. I would not have believed it myself, except I have seen it in the spirit.

God showed it to me and I could not "unsee" what I had seen. *"For we cannot but speak the things which we have seen and heard* (Acts 4:20)." Here is what I wrote in a blog one morning after prayer. *"Today, I was awaken in the wee hours of the morning to pray in the spirit. As I prayed, my eyes were opened to see what appeared to be the Spirit of Baal in a vision. He had a monstrous face. There was fire in his mouth. An infant was being placed in his mouth. When I prayed, he disappeared. He vanished. Moments later he appeared again, continuing to devour babies. It was as though he could not be stopped. Someone in authority over our nation had given this demonic entity license to kill our babies . . . What I saw in prayer this morning was not done by human beings. It was supernatural. We prayed and God heard our prayers. He honored His Covenant and sent the angels to prevail in our favor. Both Baal and Jezebel were expelled from the nation, as the leaders who worship them were removed. This was not done by human power. This was done by Almighty God and His Glory moving upon His people. And, I just heard another word in the realm of the spirit. "The devil thought he had us. He cannot stop God." In fact, I saw a glimpse of what's coming. I saw what God promised coming to pass quickly because of what the devil did. Sin increased in America, but God's grace towards us has abounded unto His Greatness."*[2] Beloved, we are in a season in which God has opened *"a great and effectual door"* for the faithful among His people. However, there are *"many adversaries* (I Corinthians 16:9)." This is not a season for the weak. Listen, anyone can be saved. All it takes is receiving Jesus Christ as the Lord of your life. But, to walk in the fullness of God's Blessing in this season, one must consecrate to the Lord. That means yielding fully to the Lord and His will. That means doing what Jesus did by *laying down His life* (John 10:15)

---

2   Matthews, Paula. Let's Talk Prophecy, Spirit & Life Publications, 22 Feb. 2022, https://www.letstalkprophecy.com/the-lord-he-is-god/. Accessed 28 July 2022.

for us. God is looking for *"a life for a Life."* Jesus sowed his Life in this earth so that God could reap a harvest of lives in this earth. That means *"a life for a Life."* God is not asking for just any type of life, but a sanctified, holy, righteous life. That is what God required of Gideon. That means tearing down *"familial altars"* and going up against the established order of evil and religion that our elders have built.

We saw this in the life of the young prophet Jeremiah. God sent him to the kingdom families of Jerusalem and Judah to utter judgment against them. The Lord said to Jeremiah, *"Be not afraid of their faces; for I am with thee to deliver thee, saith the Lord. Then the Lord put forth his hand, and touched my mouth. And the Lord said unto me, Behold, I have put my words in thy mouth. See, I have set thee over the nations and over the kingdoms to root out, and to pull down, and to destroy, and to throw down, and to build, and to plant* (Jeremiah 1:8-10)." Take note that believers are expected to build and plant what God desires for His Kingdom. However, before we can plant something, the ground must be tilled. We have to remove what has already been planted by the evil one. The bad trees must be *rooted out*. They must be *pulled down* and *destroyed*. This is what a successful farmer does before sowing seeds in the ground. The ground must be tilled. Everything that could choke and kill the seed must be removed. That is how it is in God's Kingdom. We have to *"root out"* before we can plant and build. This process can be very painful.

When the Lord spoke to me about entering into the promise this season, the first thing He required was for me to **"break family curses."** He sent me on a three day fast to break: (1) Every altar of wickedness, (2) Evil covenants made by us, or our ancestors on our behalf, and (3) Generational curses that have resulted from these evil covenants. The Lord took me to Deuteronomy Chapter 7 to explain why it was important to break these evil covenants and curses. When the Children of Israel were released from slavery in Egypt, God sent them into the wilderness on their way to possess their promised land. God explained that the land they were to inherit was being inhabited by *"seven nations"* that were stronger and mightier than they were. In order to take down the giants and take the land, God's people had to follow His instructions. God promised to deliver the enemies in the land into their hands. They were then required to kill the enemy. They were told to show them no mercy and make no covenants with them, not even covenants of marriage. Because we didn't know better, our lives have been *"intermingled with the enemy"* for generations. Our forefathers married into some demonic stuff. Now, to possess the land and keep it, we have to clean it all up. Which in the natural seems like an impossible task. How does one destroy all the works of the devil from all the generations since Adam? *"With men this is impossible; but with God all things are possible* (Matthew 19:26)."

God's instruction concerning how to deal with the evil inhabitants of the land was quick simple. *"Ye shall destroy their altars and break down their images, and cut down their groves, and burn their graven images with fire* (Deuteronomy 7:2-5)." In our day, we have a better covenant. We don't have to kill our enemies. Also, we may never see their altars or images to destroy them. Under our blood covenant, we need only to speak and obey the word of God in order to destroy the enemies squatting on our promise. For me to **"break family curses"** it began with fasting and prayer. Even after those three days, the process continues. When the Lord told me to write this book, I learned that deliverance is a process; not a one time event. The higher we go in the Kingdom, the more consecration that is required. As we receive the greater glory, we must confront the great evil that hinders us. According to the Lord, fasting and prayer would **"Break every yoke of bondage"** that is preventing us from walking in the **"Authenticity"** of God's word and destiny for our lives.

Familial altars have resulted in generational curses in the human blood line. In Christ, we have a new Blood line. Yet, we must apply the Blood of Jesus, through the word of faith. When we hear the voice of the Spirit and obey it, we are walking in covenant. We are walking in the Blood of Jesus. No rituals are required. Only obedience to the word and instruction of the Spirit of the Lord. God's covenant is **"conditional."** He will deliver His promises, if we *"hearken"* to His voice to obey (Deuteronomy 28:1). It's very important to destroy familial altars. They are a point of contact with the supernatural. If you know a person who has lost a loved, they can make an altar from a picture, or a song. It could be a favorite meal that they shared. Whatever is being used to connect with the realm of the spirit is considered an altar. I've been in homes where someone had died and the presence of the person is still in the house. The surviving spouse refused to let go of the person. They still fix meals for them. They continue having conversation with them in their favorite chair. On the surface, this looks like normal grief, but it is really an altar being used to communicate with the dead. Unfortunately, that loved one has passed. That which they are communicating with is a demon whose sole purpose is to **"lure"** the surviving person to hell. Even though the surviving person longs to reconnect with the one who passed, this opens up a portal to hell. Let me explain how I know. One of my first experiences in hell was a wild ride. I ended up in the place where the Lord said, **"the false prophets"** get their knowledge. It was a very strange place. It looked real, but there was something very odd about it. It was surreal. People were walking and talking in this realm, but they were not real. I know this sounds strange, but this is my interpretation of what I saw during that trip to hell. Then I saw a figure that looked like a relative of mine who had died years before. Except, it wasn't her. And, when I turned around to get another glimpse of her, that figure turned into a demon what looked at me and grinned sheepishly. Nothing in that realm was real. I understand why some people might be fooled into believing that it was real. People were walking, but they were like "hologram" figures.

Now imagine, if this is where the devil's people are getting their information, no wonder they are so convinced that it is real. They have nothing to compare it to. A child of God who has seen and experienced the "real deal" spiritually cannot be fooled by the false. Then there are witchcraft altars, created when people want to get revenge on another. Strife, jealousy and envy become the conduits for every evil work of the devil (James 3:16). They also get their information from this realm. This is why we must make sure our hearts are aligned with God when entering into the realm of the spirit. If not, we could be easily fooled. The Bible tell us to test the spirits to see if they are of God. *"Beloved, do not believe every spirit, but test the spirits, whether they are of God; because many false prophets have gone out into the world* (I John 4:1)." Any spirit that does not confess that Jesus is Lord, is not of God. In our world, there is a battle going on where God's prophets and the false prophets are speaking the will of their gods. People really have to be close to God, in His word and in prayer to be able to discern the truth from a lie.

God also requires of His people an increased level of sanctification. As we are elevated in Christ, it is required that we consecrate ourselves. It's one thing to be promoted by the Lord. It's another thing to be able to achieve an elevation in faith and remain steadfast in that position. Deliverance is an ongoing process. We move from *"faith to faith* (Romans 1:17)," and from one level of glory to the next (II Corinthians 3:18). There is an odd verse that appears twice in the Bible, in which God told His people that He would not destroy the enemy all at once. *"And the Lord thy God will put out those nations before thee by little and little: thou mayest not consume them at once, let the beast of the field increase upon thee* (Deuteronomy 7:22)." Their deliverance and possession of the land was gradual because God's people were too few in number. I truly believe that this New Kingdom Era will bring about something remarkably different from the past. Of the billions people on the planet, I believe that God could in an instance, transform the hearts of billions of souls, even in a day. It is God's will that all men be saved and come into the knowledge of the truth (I Timothy 2:4). Not all will come to the Lord. However, God only needs is a remnant to fulfill His will for the earth.

The Lord is a **"military strategist."** His methods are ever changing, while His will remains the same. That is why it is necessary to hear God's voice and follow His instructions. He knows every plot, scheme, and roadblock of the devil. He knows how to navigate us through the darkness into our destiny. To hear His voice requires that we put away all other voices; those of our past, those of our parents and ancestors who are directing us to follow them instead of following God. Let me remind you that God said, we are at **"the end of the last days."** We have to wrap this thing up quickly. If our ancestors ways could sufficed, then God would have no need of us in this hour. It would have already been done. God spoke to me about this ever so clearly. We have been warned. We love our parents. We honor them, but their time has ended. The past is gone. Again, the Lord said that **"the works of man has ended."** We have entered a New Era where everything must be done in the supernatural. Never in my life have I seen so much witchcraft in business and government. The devil's kids are out of the closet. There is no shame in their game. They are open about whom they serve. What about Christians? So many have shrunk back in fear of being persecuted.

God gave me this warning, as I was taking a moment to honor a person of accomplishment who was also a believer. The Lord said to me, **"The past is in the past. Your future is not like that which has past. It's a new era with new leaders and greater motivation." "New leadership has emerged." "Don't mark your future by what has passed."** The Lord said this to me because I could have built an altar for success based upon what this person of merit had done in their lifetime. Not all altars are intended to be evil, but they are wicked, meaning "twisted," and out of line with God's will.

According to the Bible, *"evil"* and *"wicked"* are from the same Hebrew word *"rah"*[3] which means bad, evil, wicked, not pleasing to God. Stop! That is all we need to know. Whether an altar is wicked or just plain evil, neither is pleasing to God! We are to worship God. Him alone shall we serve with all our heart, our mind, soul and strength. For a Christian to do otherwise brings about the curse upon their lives. Heathens live in the curse. They don't know what it is to be holy and righteous before God. It's not in their thoughts. However, if we call ourselves Children of God, then we ought to imitate Him like dear children (Ephesians 5:1). That means putting away all other idols. Destroying those altars and erecting one in our hearts to the True and Living God. Forget about tradition. Forget about what worked in the past. Forget the altars and pledges from fraternities and sororities, to unknown Greek gods. Forget even the secret societies that make you pledge to men and women who are carrying evil spirits.

Familial altars bring about familiar spirits that tie our souls to demons. Those demons serve only to turn your heart away from God, causing you to forfeit your inheritance in Christ. Even more than that. The devil uses familiar spirits to *"lure"* people into hell. That's the bottom line with the devil. He does not want you to possess the land. He doesn't want you to do anything that glorifies God. So, he **distracts** you with a title or a position. Or, he **distracts** you with a fantasy; about a life that will never happen. The devil is a thief who comes only to steal, kill and destroy. The same applies to people who make satanic altars to marry other people against their will. At some point, the potion wears off and the charm refuses to work. Every last bit of it is against God's will. Marriage is a sacred institution between two consenting adults. It's not about sex, domination or control. It's about righteousness. It's about a family coming together to receive a godly inheritance in the earth.

Tear down those evil altars in the name of Jesus. I hear the Lord saying that **"Some of you have a vision board filled with pictures of people and things that God did not ordain for your lives."** Tear them down now. In the realm of the spirit, the Lord is showing me scrapbooks of pictures of movies stars and entertainers. Leave those people alone. Let them go! That's not God! You cannot make a person your husband or wife. You are messing with their divine destiny! Let them go in the Name of Jesus! I also hear the Lord say, *"a life for a life."* If you take their lives in fantasy, then you are aborting

---

[3] H7451 - ra' - Strong's Hebrew Lexicon (kjv). Retrieved from https://www.blueletterbible.org/lexicon/h7451/kjv/wlc/0-1/

your own life. That is exactly what the devil wants you to do. He wants you to destroy your own life!!! Whatever you do for, or against another person's life, will also happen to you. This is the law of seedtime and harvest at work once again. So, leave people alone! Let them go! Tear down those *"familial altars"* of fantasy! Repent! Repent now! Then get in prayer and ask God to reveal to you what is rightfully yours.

Renounce every covenant you made with those demon spirits in an attempt to take that other person into your life. Your altar opened the door for demons to be sent to that other person. Did you ever wonder why so many entertainers in Hollywood are screwed up? Most of it is from demons that fans send their way. Those demons are wrecking people's lives just like the devil designed. Let God be god in that person's life. What you are doing is witchcraft! You cannot make another person obey you without taking away their liberty! Who died and made you God? Let them go! In the Name of Jesus!

I also want to send this strong warning to every witch out there! Your time is UP! God is about to invade your space in a way that HE WILL NOT BE DENIED! I have seen this in the spirit many times. So many of you turned to witchcraft looking for love, others for power. That devil lied to you. He lured you into a trap in order to get you killed. Repent! You have set in motion a series of curses that are about to turn an evil harvest upon you and your loved ones. Repent right now! Give your life to Jesus Christ and let Him navigate you through the pain and suffering that is heading your way. Many of you did not know. Other simply didn't care. They would have done evil all the way to hell without remorse. But not you!!! Stop and repent today! God will forgive you, no matter what you have done. He already knows about it. Why not come clean today and destroy every evil altar in your home, your office or ritual room. Burn every image, book, talisman, anything used in your rituals. Ask the Lord to show you what else must be destroyed. Sweep that place clean! Some of you may have to move, especially if others are still practicing in your midst. Let the Lord lead you to freedom. Let Him shower you with His love. Let Him demonstrate His power in your life. God is a loving Father who is quick to deliver His own. All He desires is for you to turn back to Him with an earnest heart. If you are ready, to turn back to God, then say the following prayer and give your life to the Lord right now.

Pray the following prayer to renounce evil covenants and curses:

Dear God,
I repent for making evil altars and following after idols and false gods of religion and the culture. I renounce every evil covenant that I made and that was made on my behalf, and that of my children, my business and anything that I possess or that is in my care. I decree with my mouth that those covenants with death are annulled and all agreements I made with hell shall not stand as I submit my allegiance to the Lordship of Jesus Christ.

Jesus, come into my heart. Cleanse me from every evil work that has come upon me, my family and all that I possess and care for. I want You to be my Lord and Savior. Fill me with Your Holy Spirit and lead me to your perfect path for my life. I pray this all in Jesus Name. Amen.

If you prayed this prayer, you have entered into a new life in Christ. You are now a member of the family of God. That means you are an heir of God and joint heir with Jesus Christ to everything that belongs to the Father.

This not church as usual. Find a good Bible believing church, but understand that this new life in Christ is about a personal relationship with God. Love Him, which means obey His voice. Let God shower you with His love. Pray (talk to God) daily. Let the Holy Spirit direct your every step. Enjoy this new life in Christ. This will prove to be the best decision of your life!

CONCLUSION

From The Curse To The Blessing

We have been delivered from the curse. We are free to enjoy the Blessing of the Lord. So, how do get there and stay there? God gave me one simple answer. ***"Chase after Him and not after things."*** Remember how we said ***"a person enters into covenant because of their perception that someone else can supply what is lacking in their lives."*** In other words, people chase after things that others possess, but God is telling us to ***"Chase after Him."*** Matthew 6:25-33 explains. *"No man can serve two masters: for either he will hate the one, and love the other; or else he will hold to the one, and despise the other. Ye cannot serve God and mammon. Therefore I say unto you, Take no thought for your life, . . . (For after all these things do the Gentiles seek:) for your heavenly Father knoweth that ye have need of all these things. But seek ye first the kingdom of God, and his righteousness; and all these things shall be added unto you."*

Materialism is the culture of America. We celebrate those who seek after wealth, riches, position, and fame. This is covetousness and idolatry. Our worship and gratitude should be to God, the Source of every good thing. He knows that we need things in this life. However, we can find ourselves worshiping money and riches (mammon), failing to realize that God has given us richly all things to enjoy (I Timothy 6:17). There is nothing more pathetic than to hear a person say, "What do I need God for, I have money." Really? Can your money protect you from sickness and disease? Can your money prevent your loved ones from being killed by a random act of violence? You can buy all the security in the world, and it won't protect you against the power of the satanic forces that are ruling the atmosphere around you. This is why we need God. His covenant provides for a Blessing with a protection plan. What God gives us, no man can take from us. If they try, they will contend with the Almighty and it won't go well for them. God protects His kids. He is a *"good Father"* but we must be grateful.

Parents, think about this. How does it make you feel when the only thing your children want from you is money and things? What if they never thank you? What if they refuse to spend time, or even talk to you? How does that make you feel? You may ignore it for a while, but then anger and resentment may set in. You're working hard to take care of those kids and they appreciate nothing you do for them. You may be tempted to cut them off. God forbid, that the Heavenly Father would ever do such to us. But, if anyone would have a reason to cut us off, it would be God. I am very grateful that God is a loving and compassionate Father who would never cut us off. However, when we step out from under His covenant to do our own thing, we cut ourselves off from His provision and protection. God will give us warnings before that happens. He knows how to jerk the slack out of our chains, *if* we are in relationship with Him. God did it with me. In fact, He has done it with me on more than one occasion. This is how I know I belong to Him. The Holy Spirit will convict us until we straighten up right.

Pardon me while I talk about Paula for a moment. Like Jesus, I learned obedience by what I suffered (Hebrews 5:8). Thank God, I learned to heed the warnings and make the right turns before danger took me out. It came close many times. One thing I had to learn was how to forgive those who repeatedly hurt me. I recall one holiday season that I became very ill. There was no warning. It just came upon me suddenly after dinner one night. I asked the Lord what was going on. He told me that I was holding something in my heart against someone. My unforgiveness had opened the door for the curse to come take my life. When the Lord identified the person, He let me know that what the person did to me reconnected to a similar incident that happened in my childhood. The Lord gave me no details on that childhood trauma, but still I had to forgive the person who hurt me. When I did, my healing came immediately. Unforgiveness is a serious thing to God. Jesus gave His life to forgive us our sins, and yet we still refuse to forgive others? The Bible is clear. If we don't forgive, God won't forgive us (Matthew 6:14-15). Notice that in my case, the unforgiveness had to do with something from my childhood. I didn't know it was there. It was buried within my soul.

The Bible says that our soul (mind, will, emotions, intellect, imagination) is **"the gateway"** to our wellbeing in this life. God wants us to prosper. He wants us to be in health, even as our soul prospers (III John 2). Our prosperity begins in the soul. I know what it's like being called to the Blessing, but living the curse in my soul. I read about good things in the Bible, but didn't know how to manifest them in my life. I didn't know whether God would give those good things to me or not. I didn't know anyone possessing those things. People told me that not everyone qualified and if I didn't see them in my life, it wasn't for me. Still, there was something within me that refused to believe what others were telling me. These were the mindsets and attitudes from my past that were keeping me locked into the curse. In my heart, I wanted to prove that God's Blessing was for me. I began pursuing God, but I also needed to have my mind renewed (Romans 12:2). So, God moved me two thousand miles away from those voices that tried to keep me in the curse. This is also what God had to do with Abraham before He could Bless him (Genesis 12:1). In that new place I gained a whole new perspective on what God was offering me. He wasn't offering things and happiness. God was offering all of Himself. Things and happiness were just part of the package. Deliverance also came as part of the package. Once I receive all of Who God was, then my desires were fulfilled. I learned that by placing God at the center of my life, all those good things just showed up.

This was definitely a change in perspective for me. I wanted to live in the Blessing, but all I needed was the Lord. It is God who is Blessed forever. Even now, if the Blessing is not flowing, I know it's not God. It's me. Paula let our relationship slip. The symptoms are obvious. If it's lack, then strife has entered the picture because I took my mind off of God. If sickness shows up, its because I stopped doing what God told me to do. It's easy to be caught up in the day to day realities of life and forget about God. This is especially true for those of us who think that because we are doing ministry work that it qualifies as relationship with God. This is no different than the hardworking father and husband who is so busy putting food on the table that he spends no time with his family. He may think he has fulfilled his duty in the family relationship. Not so! His family would rather have him sit down and enjoy their time together. That's what God expects from all of His kids, and especially those who are in the Family business. No matter who we are, we must *"cultivate"* our relationship with God. This is our greatest duty as a believer. Jesus said it was our greatest commandment. *"Thou shalt love the Lord thy God with all thy heart, and with all thy soul, and with all thy mind* (Matthew 22:37)." We must love God first and foremost. If we get this relationship right, everything else will fall into place. It's God first, and the Blessing follows. Therefore, if we are not living in the Blessing, it's not God's fault. It's ours. We have to follow the rules. That means that we have to forgive. We have to obey God's instructions for our lives. Everything flows from our relationship with God. Here's personal example. Under the Blessing, money flows out of my spirit. It's an anointing that I carry. It's like I am birthing money in the realm of the spirit. Some people can tell when it's going to rain by the aches in their joints. I can tell if it's about "to rain" money. The spirit on the inside of me raises up in my belly like a tsunami wave. My response is always the same. "Thank you Jesus, money is coming to me now." Within a short period later, money is either in my hand, or someone calls to say that it's on the way. That same anointing also comes upon me for others as well. I couldn't conjure up such a sensation if I tried. When that wave comes out of my belly I began releasing wealth upon those around me. It's another form of prophetic utterance that usually comes with fairly immediate results.

When I don't sense that wave, I still rely on my faith, especially when the Lord is telling me to make purchases for which I don't have the funds. For example, my corporate budgets are beyond imaginations. God is propelling me beyond anything that I could ever ask, think or imagine (Ephesians 3:20). I must be careful to surround myself with people of *"like-minded faith."* Small-minded people tend to strive against the things of God. We are called to possess the land. Small-minded people see themselves like grasshoppers (Numbers 13:33). They see those around them like grasshoppers too. Don't believe it? Try flying like an eagle. Those same people will demean and mock you enough to make you stay on the level of a grasshopper. These are people who hate the fact that you are Blessed. If you get into strife with them, it will only hinder your Blessing. In fact, it will open the door for the curse to overtake the Blessing.

Recently, I had to make a purchase for which I had no funds. My budget was depleted and the purchase had to be made rather quickly. I prayed and the Lord told me to start by purchasing part of what I needed. Still, I would have to wait for money to come before purchasing the remainder, but in my spirit I knew that I needed to act immediately. I prayed about what to do. I found something that "I could afford" when more money came in. It was not good enough. Then one night the Lord told me to upgrade my purchase to another product that was twice as expensive. The Holy Spirit was prompting me to act immediately. That night I could not sleep. I knew that if the Holy Spirit was prompting me, then there had to be something that I could do now. I prayed and went back searching online. Finally, I found something from a reputable supplier I have used faithfully over the past ten plus years. They offered me payments without interest for the remainder of the year. I had just enough cash on hand pay the down payment. So, I placed my order. The moment I did, the tsunami wave began to flow out of my belly again. It flowed that night, the next morning and the days that followed. Here's is what the Holy Spirit revealed. Certain people were intentionally speaking evil over my finances. They had already determined what <u>they thought</u> I could afford. It took an act of faith on my part to break that curse and let the money flow again. From that one act, other things began to flow again. Creative ideas that I could not complete, were energized. All of a sudden revelation began to flow. Doors were reopened and more money began to flow. The Lord also began giving me "next level" business plans. He said it was time to ***"move forward!"*** Weeks before all this happened God took me back to the Blessing in Deuteronomy 28. He told me to meditate on the Blessing daily. Even in my sleep, I could hear those words ringing out of my spirit. It's one thing to break family curses and renounce the evil covenants. It's another thing to erase the memory tapes and replace them with new scripts based on the Blessing. If all people say about you is evil, what do you do? If all that you say about yourself is also evil, what can you do? We must make a choice of whom we choose to believe? Do we believe God, or the voices from the past? It takes a concerted effort to speak the life in those places where the curse has been prevalent. The devil will remind you of your failures. He'll put shame on you to keep you from moving forward. If you can get past the shame and the blame of the devil, you can enjoy God's Blessing for your life.

Listen, if you want to be Blessed, you may have to stand alone, you and God. You'll soon learn that not everyone will be happy for the Blessing in your life. Those who are most envious may be prone to hurl biting comments at you. They may even mock what God is doing through you. Stand boldly. God knows where you came from. His Grace is sufficient (II Corinthians 12:9) for you. God does not use perfect people. He uses those who are **"perfectly yielded to His plan and purpose for their lives."** So, get over yourself. Gideon was greatly used by God and he considered himself the least of his family. I know what it's like to have family put you down and try to lock you in a box for life. They may still be in the curse and expect the generations to remain there. That's on them. Someone in the bloodline has to show them that there is something else available in life. **"Chase after God."** God is desperately seeking those who will make Him famous in the earth. Remember that the purpose of the Blessing is to *set us up on high above all nations* (Deuteronomy 28:1), yet it's not really about us. It's about the God that we serve. It's about the benefits that are available to those who would *hearken* to His Voice. God wants His people to be above only and not beneath. In other words, God wants to set us apart (holy) unto Himself. He wants to make a difference between His people and those in the world (Exodus 11:7). God wants us to be an example of what it's like to be a member of His Royal Family. Someone has to demonstrate the Kingdom way of living, if the world is to take notice. Consider this one thing. When a celebrity endorses a product, it is because that advertiser wants to influence you into buying that product. Think about how much time, money and effort goes into creating a television commercial. Companies spend billions of dollars trying to sell you a product, an idea or a lifestyle. Why? Advertising works. Public Relations programs work.

Think about the Church of Jesus Christ in America. We, the people of God have done a poor job of advertising the Kingdom. The Apostle Paul talks about how we are *"ambassadors for Christ* (II Corinthians 5:20)." We have been given the *"word of reconciliation"* but what have we really reconciled back to God and His Kingdom? We have tried to tie people down with religious tradition that has nothing to do with the Kingdom. We have compromised and let the world direct our works. God has given us the authority and instruction to bring the world under Kingdom subjection. In other words, we have been delinquent in our duties. Why? We view God as religion. We view His Blessing as something that comes in the "after life" and not in this life. Rather than going after the Kingdom, we follow after everything that the world advertises as *"good," "profitable," "pleasant to the senses"* and *"desirable to make one wise* (Genesis 3:6)." Sounds familiar doesn't it? This is how the serpent "deceived" Eve in the garden. He used *demonic* advertising. It was deceptive, but advertising just the same. The devil saw a desire in the woman and developed a strategy to steal the Blessing by selling her **"snake oil."** The devil is a thief. Listen to how Jesus described the devil. *"He was a murderer from the beginning, and abode not in the truth, because there is no truth in him. When he speaketh a lie, he speaketh of his own: for he is a liar, and the father of it* (John 8:44)." That devil wants to destroy our divine destiny. He's a murderer. He twists the truth of God and turns it into a lie. To stay under the Blessing we must learn how to discern the truth from a lie. Jesus said, *"If ye continue in my word, [then] are ye my disciples indeed; And ye shall know the truth, and the truth shall make you free* (John 8:31-32)." God's word is truth (John 17:17). If we continue in God's word, we will know the truth and that truth will make us free from the traps of the enemy. We must develop a desire for truth. Otherwise the enemy will deceive us and the curse will take prevalence in our lives.

We're talking about how to go from the curse to the Blessing and remain there. One must be diligent to go after God's plan for our lives (Jeremiah 29:11). Jesus restored us back to God's plan of peace and not evil. Contrast this with the plan the devil has for your life. He wants to do all in his power to keep God's plan from manifesting in our lives. This is a battle over divine destiny. We who have been born again into the image and likeness of God, must find, and fulfill our God given destiny. This is bigger than the Blessing or the curse. It's the purpose for which Jesus died, resurrected and ascended on High. Satan fights the full gospel message. He knows the power it has to transform a lives. This is why it is necessary for the Church of Jesus Christ to demonstrate the power of the Kingdom. We should be advertising the message of the Kingdom through word and demonstration, just like Jesus did. Unfortunately, many Christians are concentrating on going to Heaven and getting out of this earthly mess. God's plan is for us to stay here and clean up the mess with the Blessing! Very few people are teaching this message. Therefore most Christians are estranged from God's true purpose and the Blessing is not flowing in their lives.

Ignorantly, many Christians find themselves living in the curse. The Blessing is our portion. In fact, it is on us. It's just not operating as it should. This was one of the greatest revelations of my life. I was "blessed" by America's standard, which included a good education, a family, marriage, home, bank account and the works. That is what we call "blessed" in America, but it's not God's definition of being Blessed. I would read Deuteronomy 28 and wonder why it wasn't happening in my life. People would call me "spoiled" because I wanted to have a better life. I wanted the life that God said I could have. Christians that I knew became very angry at me. Who did I think I was? Who told me I could have a better life than they had? Who told me? God told me in His word. As a youngster, I read Deuteronomy 6:10-11 and those words echoed in my heart. *"And it shall be, when the LORD thy God shall have brought thee into the land which he sware unto thy fathers, to Abraham, to Isaac, and to Jacob, to give thee great and goodly cities, which thou buildedst not, And houses full of all good [things], which thou filledst not, and wells digged, which thou diggedst not, vineyards and olive trees, which thou plantedst not . . ."* No one told me that God did such things for people. I read it in the Bible. Those words have stuck with me even to this very day. That Bible provided the proof that I needed, that God had something better than what I was witnessing in the lives of those around me.

I became a *"God chaser,"* and it upset people. In many ways, it still does. Instead of chasing after our God and letting things *"overtake"* us, we chase after things just like the world does. Then when we achieve what the world deems as success we call it the "blessing" of the Lord. Well, the Blessing of the Lord is *"a flow."* We don't make it happen. We simply follow the leading of the Holy Spirit and the Blessing flows without toil or sorrow. There are too many "blessed" Christians who are toiling with sickness and death, just like the world. They have a reasonable amount of success, but they are not lending to nations. They are striving to be on top, but they are not *"high above all the nations of the earth."* Until they follow God, the Blessing of the Lord will not flow. They will find themselves in the curse. Oh, they may have stuff, but it will come with much pain, sorrow and grief. That is why the wealthy in America are plagued with excessive sex, drugs and other addictions. It's the only way they can cope with the sorrow. When that does not work, many turn to suicide.

We said from the beginning that people enter into covenants because they want things. They will even make evil covenants simply because they want things. Earlier in this book, I spoke about a woman who "just had to have that man." She turned her back on God and found herself in a crazy relationship. This was exactly what the devil wanted her to do. I don't know what ever happened to her, but I know the man brought drugs and more occult practices into her life. Yet she went after him. It was her choice. Her focus was not on God, but on her own happiness. As if, God isn't concerned about our happiness. That is what the Blessing is about. *"Praise ye the LORD. Blessed [is] the man [that] feareth the LORD, [that] delighteth greatly in his commandments* (Psalm 112:1)." That word Blessed is translated "happy."[1] We often associate the word blessed with physical things, but the Bible defines Blessed as "happy, happiness." This is a much different interpretation than what many would think. *"Blessed [Happy] is the man that walked not in the counsel of the ungodly, nor standeth in the way of sinners, nor sitteth in the seat of the scornful. But his delight [is] in the law of the LORD; and in his law doth he meditate day and night. And he shall be like a tree planted by the rivers of water, that bringeth forth his fruit in his season; his leaf also shall not wither; and whatsoever he doeth shall prosper* (Psalm 1:1-3)." From this scripture we can see that a "happy" person according to God's standards, *prospers* in all that they do. To be cursed is the opposite of being "happy" and *prosperous*. A curse brings pain, bitterness and adversity

---

1   H835 - 'ešer - Strong's Hebrew Lexicon (kjv). Retrieved from https://www.blueletterbible.org/lexicon/h835/kjv/wlc/0-1/

upon ones life. People who curse others are not trying to make their lives happy. They want people to suffer. That is why people curse others. However, God does not want us to suffer. The curse comes because we have set things in motion to warrant a curse. We must let people go. We must forgive. When we go after people whether intentionally or not, we encounter the curse. We must let go and let God handle people. Otherwise, we open the door for the enemy to attack our bodies, our minds and every aspect of our lives. The curse is never God's plan for us. It's our choice.

Take the woman who went to the herbalist for a potion and a charm. This woman, like so many of us, fell prey to the snake oil sells man who lured her away from the happiness (Blessings) of God into a "pseudo" happiness that resulted in pain and sorrow. The devil is always on his job. He comes to steal, kill and destroy our happiness. Yet he cannot do it outright. He has to *"lure"* us into the curse with deception. The devil comes to kill our dreams from God. That deceiver comes to destroy our faith and hope in God, but he cannot do it without our permission. Oh Believer, You have been given dominion. The devil deceived you out of your authority for the moment. Take it back by annulling evil covenants and breaking those curses. Repent. That means stop doing what you are doing and change direction. Stop chasing people and things. **"Chase after God."**

Follow God. *"Ye shall not do after all [the things] that we do here this day, every man whatsoever [is] right in his own eyes (Deuteronomy 12:8)."* We are commanded not to go after the things as the world does. That is the **"wrong focus"** for the believer. The enticement is to go after things. That is what the world does because they don't know God. This should never be said about the Body of Christ. God knows that we have need of things. That is why the Blessing includes things, but it's not about acquiring things. It's about cultivating a relationship with God from whom all Blessings flow. It's the difference between going directly to the Source of Life to get the things we need, versus going to a **"middle man deceiver"** who is trying to make a profit off of us. Cut out the middle man of sin and you will get the **"legitimate goods,"** from the Source which is God, the Creator of all good things. Now, there are some things in the world that look good, but they have been **"laced with the curse."** They look like the real deal, but they are a set up to kill you. That is the purpose of satan. He not only wants to deceive you, but His ultimate purpose is to kill and destroy you. The devil purposely **"lures"** people into decisions that are against God's will for their lives. That is what he did to Eve in the garden. He observed her interest in something and used it to lure her to sin against God. Some of you may be asking, "If the devil can so easily lure us into the curse, how do we get to the Blessing?" It takes *"discernment,"* not just discerning the spirits that are working through people, but being able to discern good from evil. It takes the wisdom of God to be able to discern things in this world accurately. Common sense and logic are based upon human ability and reason. They are no match against the evil one. It takes spiritual knowledge to outsmart the devil. Some people don't like working that hard. They prefer to take a person or situation as they see it. However, deception is every where. It's all around us. That is what the Lord showed me in the *vision* of snakes. They were everywhere. For one to obtain the Blessing it takes being in tune with the Holy Spirit, who guides us into *all truth* (John 16:13). Now, the assumption is that you desire to know the truth, otherwise, the Blessing is not for you.

People are also self-deceived. They simply don't want to know the truth. Therefore they are in delusion, but that's their choice. Truth scares some people. It forces them to make changes that they don't want to make in their lives. It's like they know the truth, but don't want admit it. It becomes fear of the truth. Therefore God's word has no place in that person's life. Because God's word is truth. The Holy Spirit is the Spirit of Truth (John 16:13). Jesus said, I am the Truth (John 14:6). This may be offensive to some, but Jesus is the <u>only</u> way to the Blessing that Adam had in the Garden of Eden. Jesus restored it for all who would believe and receive. It's the inheritance that God set aside for all of His earthly children. So what if people have a problem with Jesus being *"the only way"* to God. It's God's inheritance. If we want it, we must follow His instructions. Think about what it means to receive an inheritance. An heir is required to provide legal evidence of their identity before they can receive an inheritance. The same is true with God. You must have proof that you are His heir through salvation. The Bible tells us the kind of proof we will have as a child of God. *"For as many as are led by the Spirit of God, they are the sons of God. For ye have not received the spirit of bondage again to fear; but ye have received the Spirit of adoption, whereby we cry, Abba, Father. The Spirit itself beareth witness with our spirit, that we are the children of God: And if children, then heirs; heirs of God, and joint-heirs with Christ* (Romans 8:14-17)." Here is the proof that you are an heir of God. First of all, you are led by His Spirit. We learned from the Blessing in Deuteronomy 28 that to be Blessed one must *"hearken diligently unto the voice of the LORD thy God, to observe and to do all his commandments."* Next, proof that you are God's heir is that you are no longer in bondage to fear. Think about it. Fear is a spirit. It does not come from God (II Timothy 1:7). Fear comes from the evil one. Finally, it is the recreated spirit that cries *"Abba"* [which means daddy]. We, who are saved have received the Spirit of adoption, being reborn of God's Spirit. These proofs are undeniable in the realm of the spirit. They will confirm your identity in Christ.

Go back to our example of the execution of a will. Let's consider what else is typically required. Once your identity is established the executor must make sure you have fulfilled specific conditions. For example, the will might specify that you receive an inheritance only after reaching a certain age. It might state that you must not be married, or even that you must reside in a specific location. You may not like the terms of the will, but you understand that this is the Last Will And Testament of the Testator. Same is true of God who has both the Old and New Testaments. This is God's Will for our lives. Therefore, His provisions in His Will must be met before an inheritance can be obtained. The will is a covenant. It is for the most part a binding agreement. People have contested wills in probate court. However that is not the case with God's Will. It is final. Don't be judgmental when Jesus tells you that He is the only Way to God. He's just telling you the legal condition stated in God's Will. We either abide by it or not. We either receive the inheritance or not, but we cannot change what God has put in His Will.

Again, it's not about the stuff. God told us by His Spirit to **"Chase after Him"** and not after things. As heirs of God, we must perform His Will, not our own. First and foremost, it is God's will that all men be saved and come into the knowledge of the truth (I Timothy 2:4). However, not all will be saved. Many will not come to the truth. Some men love darkness and won't acknowledge the truth because they want to continue doing evil (John 3:19). That's their choice, but for those who want to live and walk in Light (truth), Jesus is the only way. It's God's truth that makes us free. If you don't love truth, don't kid yourself. You will never be free. Truth is the great liberator of mankind. God also pursues those who pursue the truth. These **"truth seekers"** will always find answers that the rest of the world will never know. Truth seekers will also be the ones *most likely* to obtain God's inheritance. I said *most likely* because by seeking the truth they place themselves in position to qualify for God's inheritance. Yet, obedience is the key. To receive and acknowledge the truth is one thing. To walk in that truth is another thing. When one chases after God, they will find truth. What they do with that truth, will determine whether or not they will be rewarded or not. One must be courageous. It takes boldness to walk in truth when the world around you is in deception. People will criticize you. It takes an humble heart and tough skin to be a faithful believer amongst unbelievers. People who hate Jesus may go out of their way to be obnoxious and vengeful. It has nothing to do with you. It's all about God. Evil people will attack and curse you because of God. It may be out of envy or jealousy, but the attack is real. To walk in God's Blessing requires a strong determination to do things God's way regardless of the persecution.

It reminds me of what God told Joshua after Moses' death. *"Be strong and of a good courage: for unto this people shalt thou divide for an inheritance the land, which I sware unto their fathers to give them. Only be thou strong and very courageous, that thou mayest observe to do according to all the law, which Moses my servant commanded thee: turn not from it to the right hand or to the left, that thou mayest prosper whithersoever thou goest. (Joshua 1:6-7)."* Notice how God emphasized the importance of being strong and courageous. That is what it takes to receive the Blessing. You will have to face off with the giants; which include the fears from the past, fears of the present and future, and fears of the sons of Anak [wicked giants] that are squatting on your promise. Be prepared for a fight. You don't have to do all the work, but <u>you do</u> have to stand in obedience to what God has told you to say or do. Stay in faith. Stay in love and don't move until you see your desire come upon those enemies (Psalm 112:8).

Our inheritance is reserved in Heaven, but there is an earthly portion that is needed in order to carry out our Kingdom assignments. This puts us on a collision course with the devil. His job, is to destroy our destinies. It begins by keeping us in the dark about God's good plan for our lives. Then he will try to keep us from getting saved. Even after salvation, the devil will play games with out past sins and attempt to keep us in condemnation. This is why we must endeavor to walk in the spirit and not in the flesh (Romans 8:2). If we get past this point and decide to go after our inheritance that devil will set another distraction or diversion on our path. However, he cannot win if we stand on what God promised and refuse to back down despite his threats. This is a fight that we are destined to win. Back in 2016

God gave me a prophecy that is manifesting in our day. This is what I heard in my spirit. *"For those who are believing God, it will be a year of restoration of all things; Not just things we know about, but things that were taken from previous generations, all the way back to Adam. It's more than restoration of what we lost. It's the restoration of what was planned from the foundation of the world; the complete and total restoration of Almighty God's plan for mankind; every word God spoke will come to pass. Every plan and purpose will be realized in <u>this</u>, our final hour on earth. "All will be accomplished," says God. "And, I will do it by My Spirit; Every jot and every tittle."* God is talking about restoring everything that every believer had lost since the time of Adam. This is a generational restoration like nothing that has ever happened in the history of the world. Essentially, God is promising to treat those who are faithful *"as if sin never existed."* Let that marinate in your spirit for a moment. This is not for everybody. It's for *"those who are believing God;"* those who are steadfast in the word regardless of what is thrown their way. I am determined to be one of them. God desires to give us that which was set aside for us before foundation of the world, *"The Riches Of His Kingdom."* This is God's idea of restoration.

Let me stress that the Lord said this type of restoration will come to those *"who are believing God."* Many Christians may say that they are believing God, but are they really? Imagine what kind of faith is necessary to be able to receive back everything that was stolen from you, all the way back to Adam. That kind of faith would require that we take a stand against every generational stronghold the enemy has laid on us and our families since the fall of man. That is exactly why the Lord told me to *"break generational curses"* off of my family. It was so that we would be in position to receive this generational restoration and experience the Blessing in its fullness.

The Holy Spirit instructed me which evil covenants were at play in our lives. I annulled those evil covenants with the power of the Blood covenant of Jesus Christ. Breaking the curses required that I also renounce the devil's hold on my family and declare our allegiance to walk in obedience to God's word. Can we do that? Can we speak for our families? According to the Bible we can. *"And if it seem evil unto you to serve the LORD, choose you this day whom ye will serve; . . . but as for me and my house, we will serve the LORD* (Joshua 24:15)." This was the question that Joshua put before the people of God, asking them to chose whom they would serve. Gideon didn't have to ask the people because God came to him on behalf of the

Israel. The man saw his nation in bondage. God's people needed a miraculous deliverance from their enemies. Gideon stood in the gap for his people, regardless of what they believed, and God delivered them. Why would God go against the people, even a rebellious people? One word. Covenant. All God needs is one man, one woman, even one child to invoke the power of the covenant, and He will intervene on the behalf of a nation. This is HUGE! This is what Jesus did on behalf of the people of the entire planet. Most of the world hates God. They hate the Name of Jesus even more. Yet one man made covenant with God to save a rebellious, godless world. Gideon did the same for his nation. We can do it also, for our own nations. God will always be faithful to His covenant people, to save their nation, even a rebellious god-hating nation.

As a result of his obedience, Gideon saw the miraculous Hand of God free his people, and he became one of the Bible heroes of faith. These were the ones *"Who through faith subdued kingdoms, wrought righteousness, obtained promises, stopped the mouths of lions, quenched the violence of fire, escaped the edge of the sword, out of weakness were made strong, waxed valiant in fight, turned to flight the armies of the aliens* (Hebrews 11:32-34)." Are you ready to be Blessed? Can you **"shoulder"** the weight of Blessing? Walking by faith is not for the faint hearted. God may require that you infiltrate the territory of the giants, and take a stand for the Kingdom; against enemy forces that have never been opposed. You will have to endure hardship like a good soldier (II Timothy 2:3). Even, as a servant of the Lord, I'm under a constant battle, especially when I am in a writing season. Most people who write books can get away to some desolate location and write in peace. I don't have that choice. Whatever I write stirs up every demon around me. That devil fights me tooth and nail, trying to get me to stop writing. Nevertheless, I write, not because I want to be a writer. I write because God called me to be His **"Mouthpiece."** I am commissioned to write whatever God instructs me to write. My words are not my own. They come straight out of Heaven. That is why there is such a battle when I write. Heaven invades the earth with every word the Lord speaks and every title He commands me to write. People around me are also tormented by the demons. Therefore, I cannot live with just anyone. The anointing on my life is brutal. If you don't want to be free, don't come around me. God gives me words that are meant to set the captives free. Not many people can handle the Spirit of the Lord upon them and around them. Some religious folks will even call it the devil. Why? They have never seen God move by His Spirit. It scares them.

In many ways, the devil has attempted to use religious people to hinder God's will in my life. It's politically correct to call yourself a Christian, just as long as you don't really believe in Jesus. That devil tried to use everyone around me, including family, friends, pastors, teachers, leaders, and politicians. Most considered themselves "believers," but the truth came out when they attempted to shame me for following God. That devil used every tactic possible, trying to get me to forfeit my destiny. He used persecution, hardship, threats of death and even threats of kidnapping and killing my child. Did I fear? No, not ever! It came to me one day, that if the devil is going to such a length, if he is trying this hard to discourage me from following God, then what's on the other side of this *hardship* must be ***"MEGA!"*** Just this week, the Lord gave me a word to deliver in which He ended by saying, **"The greater the opposition, the higher the position."** In other words, don't look at what the enemy is doing as a problem. See it as your ticket to promotion. You will be promoted if you do not faint under the pressure from the evil one.

"Chasing after God" means following after Christ with all that is within you. It means denying oneself taking up your cross and following Jesus' example (Matthew 16:24). It means loving and obeying God above everyone and everything else. Submit to God above all, and you have the ability to resist the devil, and eventually, he will flee (James 4:7). Alone, we have no power to withstand the enemy who uses all the power of hell to oppose us. Indeed, Jesus gave us power to tread upon serpents, scorpions, and over all the power of the enemy (Luke 10:19), but we have to walk it out by faith. That may mean leaving loved ones behind for a season. **"Chasing after God"** led me two thousand miles away from home, to the place of my inheritance. Like Abraham, I was told to depart from my family and all that was familiar to me, and go to a land that I had never known. The Lord called it my **"Place of Restoration."** As awesome as it was to hear those words from God, I witnessed the reality of what Jesus said to his disciples about giving up everything for the Kingdom. *"Verily I say unto you, There is no man that hath left house, or brethren, or sisters, or father, or mother, or wife, or children, or lands, for my sake, and the gospel's, But he shall receive an hundredfold now in this time, houses, and brethren, and sisters, and mothers, and children, and lands, with persecutions; and in the world to come eternal life* (Mark 10:29-30)." I ask again, "Are you ready to be Blessed?" What if it means walking away from family? What if it means giving up your money and possessions? What if it means enduring hardship, mockery and shame for a season? What are you willing to risk for the glory of God's Kingdom? What are you willing to endure to be Blessed? I've often found comfort in the words of the Apostle Paul whenever I was going through hardship. *"[We are] troubled on every side, yet not distressed; [we are] perplexed, but not in despair; Persecuted, but not forsaken; cast down, but not destroyed; Always bearing about in the body the dying of the Lord Jesus, that the life also of Jesus might be made manifest in our body. For we which live are alway delivered unto death for Jesus' sake, that the life also of Jesus might be made manifest in our mortal flesh (II Corinthians 4:8-11)."* I used to call this the "knocked down but not knocked out" speech. This is how I have felt on many occasions, but then I am reminded of the sufferings of my Lord Jesus Christ. In those times I ask, "What more am I able to endure in order to manifest the glory of God in this earthen vessels of mine?" "Is it worth it?" I believe so. If given the chance, I would do it all over again [maybe with fewer trials].

Beloved, we are in a kairos moment in time. There will never be another time like the one in which we live. What we do in this season, will be written about for the ages to come. I admonish everyone to **"Chase after God"** and His destiny for your life. Go after Him with your whole heart. Encounter the greatest trials of your faith, to obtain the **"Highest"** reward reserved for mankind. *"For our light affliction, which is but for a moment, worketh for us a far more exceeding [and] eternal weight of glory; While we look not at the things which are seen, but at the things which are not seen: for the things which are seen [are] temporal; but the things which are not seen [are] eternal* (II Corinthians 4:17-18)."

Ruling And Reigning In The Kingdom

We are drawing near to the end of the age. Jesus will return soon, and there is much to be done before His arrival. What God is about to do through His people will not be Church as usual. It will be God's Kingdom in all of its power and glory as the **Ancient Kingdom Dynasty** is restored in the earth. Everything that can be shaken, will be shaken in these last days. It won't be pleasant for the enemies of God. However, the Remnant of Christ will be *"ecstatic"* because the God of Heaven will make Himself known in the earth. *"The heathen raged, the kingdoms were moved: He uttered His Voice, the earth melted* (Psalm 46:6)."

Why is the heathen raging? Why have the kings of the earth devised evil plans against the Lord and His anointed (Psalm 2:1-2)? The heathen is trying to prevent God's Kingdom from rising in the earth. Yet, God is unstoppable. It's God's appointed time to fulfill end-time prophecy. *"And in the days of these kings shall the God of heaven set up a kingdom, which shall never be destroyed: and the kingdom shall not be left to other people, [but] it shall break in pieces and consume all these kingdoms, and it shall stand for ever (Daniel 2:44)."* This is where we are in the plan of God. He's the one who created us. God is the one who determined our role in His stage production before the foundation of the world. God is in control! He wrote the script, and no man can change it. I recall *a dream in the night in which I saw The Hand of God pick up the earth as if it were a toy ball. God shook this planet with such violence that I could hear the demons screaming for mercy.* It was such a severe shaking that I woke up in horror, and ran to the window expecting to see damage in the streets. Beloved, God is overturning the wicked governments of the world. He is putting down some leaders (in the government, in business, in the Church) and setting up others to replace them (Psalm 75:7).

This will come to be known as the **"greatest transformation known to mankind."** As the prophet of Old wrote, *"But in the last days it shall come to pass, that the mountain of the house of the Lord shall be established in the top of the mountains; and it shall be exalted above the hills; and people shall flow unto it* (Micah 4:1)." In other words, in these last days, God's spiritual Kingdom will be exalted above all other kingdoms on earth. His glory will cover the earth and all the people shall see it. They will come into the Kingdom seeking to learn the ways of the Lord. How can this be done? Considering where humanity is today, it would take a great transformation for God to be exalted in the earth. The wicked kings of the earth have launched a campaign of hatred for everything that is godly. Therefore, something drastic must come to pass in order for the prophecy about God's Kingdom can come to pass. So, God is shaking the earth. We see the beginnings of it now. The kingdoms of men are falling ever so quickly. The time is soon coming when Revelation 11:15 will be fulfilled, *"The kingdoms of this world are become the kingdoms of our Lord, and of his Christ; and he shall reign for ever and ever."*

Everyone who names the Name of Jesus has a part in this transformation. God didn't deliver us from the power of darkness just so we could go to Heaven. No! God delivered us from the enemy as a demonstration of His power. *"To open their eyes, and to turn them from darkness to light, and from the power of Satan unto God* (Acts 26:18)." Our deliverance is about demonstrating the power of God's Kingdom. We have forgiveness of sins and an inheritance, however it is all for a greater purpose. *"Ask of me, and I shall give [thee] the heathen [for] thine inheritance, and the uttermost parts of the earth [for] thy possession* (Psalm 2:8)." Restoring God's Ancient Kingdom Dynasty requires that we, the children of God, take our rightful places His heirs in the earth. As we said before, we have been chosen as *"kings and priests"* to our Lord. We are a *"royal priesthood, a chosen generation;"* chosen for God's purpose, not our own. God's purpose for our lives is bigger than anything we could ever imagine. It's about ruling in the midst of our enemies. *"The LORD shall send the rod of thy strength out of Zion: rule thou in the midst of thine enemies* (Psalm 110:2)." The Lord has been ministering this to me for years. Let me explain.

It began in the summer of 2015, when the Lord said to me, **"It's time to recover all!"**[1] I recall those words from the story of David and his mighty men who returned from battle to find that their city had been burned. The women and children, and all their possessions had been taken by the enemy. David's men blamed him for what happened and wanted to take his life. The Bible says that David encouraged himself in the Lord and asked if he should go up against the enemy. God responded, *"And he answered*

---

1   Matthews, Paula. "In Pursuit Of My Inheritance." *It's Time To Recover All! Restoring God's Kingdom Dynasty On Earth*. Atlanta: Spirit & Life Publications[SM], 2016. 35. Print.

him, Pursue: for thou shalt surely overtake them, and without fail recover all* (I Samuel 30:8)." David and his men destroyed the enemy and recovered everything that was stolen. They took that which belonged to the enemy as spoils. A week later I was seated in a meeting when the Lord said to me, **"Paula, will you lead them?"** When I asked how to lead, God responded, **"Restore the dynasty on earth."** I agreed to lead God's people, not fully understanding what that meant. Then, in the spring of 2017, the Lord shook me out of bed with these words, **"The Kingdom must be delivered up!"**[2] He was not quoting scripture. This was a direct command from Heaven. Immediately I arose out of bed and got my Bible. I turned to I Corinthians 15:24-25 which reads, *"Then cometh the end, when he shall have delivered up the kingdom to God, even the Father; when he shall have put down all rule and all authority and power. For he must reign, till he hath put all enemies under his feet."* Until that morning, I had always thought this scripture was talking about Jesus coming back to deliver up the Kingdom to the Father. The Lord opened my eyes to see **"that we are seated together with Jesus in the heavenly places. We are His Body in this earth. We are called to deliver up the Kingdom. We must do it and prepare the way for our King. We must take up and finish what Jesus started. We go in His name."**

Then the Lord reminded me of everything He had called me to do. It was all brought back to me with a sense of urgency, and I saw it. Our divine destiny has to be fulfilled. We must take back the people, the land and possessions for God's Kingdom. To accomplish this monumental Kingdom assignment we must be freed from all entanglements. This is why the Lord wants us freed from evil covenants and curses. That enemy will come, but let him have no claim on us (John 14:30). We belong to God. It does not mean that we are perfect. We are far from perfect. What we have is a **"divine authority to rule and reign in Jesus' Name."** This is how the Ancient Kingdom Dynasty will be restored. What we are in the process of witnessing is more than a promise of an inheritance. It's about God's covenant with Jesus to reconcile mankind and the earth back into the Kingdom.

The great end-time wealth and power transfer is a large part of God's plan for reconciliation. Almighty God is transferring wealth and power to those whom He can trust to do His bidding in the earth. Solomon wrote, *"For God giveth to a man that is good in his sight wisdom, and knowledge, and joy: but to the sinner he giveth travail, to gather and to heap up, that he may*

---

2   Matthews, Paula. "The Blessing To Rule And Reign In Life." *Living In The Faith Zone, Locked And Loaded.* Atlanta: Spirit & Life Publications[SM], 2019. 154. Print.

give to him that is good before God. This also is vanity and vexation of spirit (Ecclesiastes 2:26)." The Lord showed this to me in a *vision. I saw the Hand of God wipe out the list of billionaires as we know them today. In one move of God, they were gone, totally wiped out. In another instance immediately following, I saw the Hand of God raise up a whole nother set of billionaires, of His choosing. There were more billionaires than before, possessing more money than those who had previously been on the list.* The wealth of the sinner will be transferred to the just (Proverbs 13:22). This does not necessarily mean it's coming to all Christians. I recall the Lord saying that the wealth and power will be given to those **"who have the heart of the Father."** These are the ones who will rule and reign in His Name. They will love what the Father loves and hate what He hates. Above all, they will operate in the love of the Father towards mankind.

Therefore, this is a season of great harvest. Whatever seeds we have sown will be coming up rather soon. We are about to witness the fall of the wicked, in the Church and in the world. God is calling for all men to repent. Those who repent will be spared from what is coming upon the earth. However, many people are distracted by what is going on in the world around them. They don't seem to realize the sign of the times. We are at **"the end of the last days."** God calls this His **"Grand Finale"** before Jesus returns. A grand finale marks the end of a production. This is normally when the plot thickens and comes to a climax. The villain is captured and the captives set free. What was stolen is returned. All cast members fill the stage singing the final medley of triumphant songs and the curtain closes. *"This coming move of God is His Grand Finale before Jesus comes; Fire in the Sky and Earth; Fireworks. It's the time of God's justice; good and bad rewarded for their persistence."*[3] God's **"Grand Finale"** has a few twists and turns.

This is God's time of justice with **"Fireworks"** to boot. What did Jesus say would happen before His return? *"And ye shall hear of wars and rumours of wars: see that ye be not troubled: for all [these things] must come to pass, but the end is not yet. For nation shall rise against nation, and kingdom against kingdom: and there shall be famines, and pestilences, and earthquakes, in divers places. All these [are] the beginning of sorrows* (Matthew 24:6-8)." All of these activities will be part of the **"*fireworks*"** going off in the earth. Think about what this passage is saying; wars among nations and king-

---

3	Matthews, Paula. "Year 2002: The Enemy Exposed And God's Plan Revealed." *The War Journal (1999-2010) Volume I.* Los Angeles: Spirit & Life Publications, 2010. 181. Print.

doms. Wars cause famines. Pestilences are the results of wars and famines. Some pestilences are used as weapons of warfare. What about earthquakes? As the striving against God increases, it shall be answered both in the earth and in the skies. Let's revisit why nations and kingdoms are striving with one another? We know that God is shaking the nations, but something else is going on as well. We go back to the prophet Daniel to explain. *"And the kingdom and dominion, and the greatness of the kingdom under the whole heaven, shall be given to the people of the saints of the most High, whose kingdom is an everlasting kingdom, and all dominions shall serve and obey him* (Daniel 7:27)." God's Kingdom *"shall be given"* to the saints. Who are the saints? They are those who have received Jesus Christ as Lord and Savior. God's Kingdom is to be given to His saints. That's not a small feat. There is a battle going on in the realm of the spirit, as God's people are in the process of obtaining their inheritances. They are taking the land for the Kingdom! This has shaken the kings of the earth. The Body of Christ is arising to take possession of the earth. The Holy Spirit called it, **"A Battle Royale: The kings of the Kingdom overcoming the kings of the earth."**

This is why the heathen is raging. Everything we have witnessed, especially since the pandemic of 2020, has been about shutting down God's plan. The lies and deception, the fraud and masquerade was all about forcing the hand of the saints to give up their divine rights in God's Kingdom. That devil even tried to convince them that man's wisdom was superior to God's. They were told to "trust the science," when science had no real answers. The reason God is judging the leaders of the nations is because they have **"severely mismanaged"** their positions in order to gain wealth for themselves. They are about to reap what they have sown. *"Go to now, [ye] rich men, weep and howl for your miseries that shall come upon [you]. Your riches are corrupted, and your garments are motheaten. Your gold and silver is cankered; and the rust of them shall be a witness against you, and shall eat your flesh as it were fire. Ye have heaped treasure together for the last days* (James 5:1-3)." Instead of accumulating wealth for themselves, they have heaped up wrath. Their treasures they have gathered, but the righteous and the just ones will possess it all in the end (Job 27:17).

For years, I've heard people preach about the wealth transfer as if it would drop out of the sky upon God's people. This is far from the truth. There is a battle raging in the earth. Whoever receives the wealth will have to conquer the demons who have it in their hands. This is not a physical fight. This is a spiritual conquest. ***"One must be fit"*** to enter into this race for wealth. The Lord showed this to me while watching a scene from the movie *"The Avengers Age of Ultron."*[4] Some of the avengers were attempting to pick up Mjolnir[Thor's hammer]. As the saying goes, whoever picks up the hammer must be found worthy. Of course, all the superheroes tried to pick it up. Only one was able to move it slightly from its position. That person was Captain America. Later in the episode, the Avenger named Vision, effortlessly picks up the hammer and hands it to Thor. These were the "good guys" who were dedicated to doing good for the sake of others. Likewise, the Lord said that not every Christian would be receiving wealth. Many are expecting to receive money, homes, cars, boats, planes, and the like. Few people understand that this wealth is not automatic. The Lord said, one ***"must be found worthy."*** It's more than a heart issue. End-time wealth requires that one is ready to fight for a righteous cause in a world that is steeped in unrighteousness.

We are kings and priests, which means that we pray, but we also to fight battles and take territories. One duty of a king is to rule over his domain (territory). God has anointed and appointed His saints to take dominion over specific regions of the earth. We were not ordained to fit into the culture. We are called to institute a new Kingdom of God culture, and occupy until Jesus comes (Luke 19:13). The Church has the responsibility of advancing the Kingdom for the cause of Christ. That means standing up for what God wants in an ungodly world. It's a tough assignment to be Light in the darkness, but it's our call. We don't compromise with the world. We don't conform to its standards. We are to over take the world system with the love and power of Almighty God. To explain this in more detail, the Lord took me to the Book of Deuteronomy, to a time just before His people were to enter into their promised land.

God took His people out of slavery in Egypt. His plan was to turn them into a mighty nation. *"And ye shall be unto me a kingdom of priests, and an holy nation* (Exodus 19:6)." God was about to raise up a *"holy nation"* in the midst of an ungodly nation. This goes back to Daniel's prophecy that God would raise a nation (kingdom) that would *"break in pieces and consume"* all other kingdoms (Daniel 2:44). Keep this in mind as we go through this discussion. The Lord takes His people out of slavery into their promise land, but before they enter in, God describes the battle that is before them.

---

4   Whedon, Josh, director. Avengers: Age of Ultron. Walt Disney Studios Home Entertainment, 2019.

"When the LORD thy God shall bring thee into the land whither thou goest to possess it, and hath cast out many nations before thee, the Hittites, and the Girgashites, and the Amorites, and the Canaanites, and the Perizzites, and the Hivites, and the Jebusites, seven nations greater and mightier than thou (Deuteronomy 7:1)." Their promise requires that they over take the enemy and possess a land that was inhabited by *"seven nations"* greater and mightier than they. How could God expect a group of former slaves to over take great nations? They were never expected to fight in this battle. The Lord promised to go before them and deliver those nations into their hands. Take note. This is the process that is required of anyone desiring to possess their inheritance from God.

Once they were in the land, God gave them specific instructions to carry out. *"And when the LORD thy God shall deliver them before thee; thou shalt smite them, [and] utterly destroy them; thou shalt make no covenant with them, nor shew mercy unto them (Deuteronomy 7:2)."* We just stated that God's Kingdom comes in order to destroy all other kingdoms. As God's people, we cannot compromise with a world that opposes Him. Fortunately, we don't have to kill people. What we are to do is sanctify the land and the people for God, by getting rid of the evil covenants and curses. Jesus Christ gave us the power to *"cast out devils (Mark 16:17)"* but we don't necessarily have to perform exorcisms because Jesus gave us *"the keys of the Kingdom."* Here is an example of how to use those keys. God had me move into a very nice condo, but there was so much demonic activity that I could not sleep. I began binding up those demonic powers and loosing the peace of God in that place. The atmosphere changed drastically over night. The next morning one of the neighbors had gotten delivered from severe demonic oppression. The demons were completely gone and the person was happy. They never knew that it was my prayer and declaration that got them free. The devil no longer had authority in that place. God had moved into the building.

Oh, Believer, you have to know that the world is having issues, but we have been given authority to solve those issue with the help of the Holy Spirit. It's time for us to arise and take dominion so that people can live in peace. If there is evil in our cities, it's because we have allowed it. If there is peace and tranquility in our cities, it's because we have released it. When the Lord gave me first *The War Journal* books, He made it clear that the issues in America were because of the **"weak and wimpy"** Church that refused to stand up against the works of the devil. It's as if they had no clue that God gave us dominion. When COVID hit the earth, God expected His people to take authority over it. We are commanded to cast out devils and lay hands on the sick, and they shall recover. But, what did the Church do? What did most Christians do? Nothing. We are His royal family ordained to rule over this earth with the Blessing. Many Christians are quick to say they are Blessed but what did God say? Let's go back to the beginning. What was the Blessing for? God Blessed them to *"be fruitful and multiply."* That is a command to **increase** in the earth. COVID came to cause mankind to decrease in the earth. It was not the Blessing. It was the curse. The Blessing causes us to *"replenish"* and *"subdue"* the earth. COVID came to cut off our fruitfulness and cause shortages in our lives. Yet, God has commanded us to *"replenish"* that which is lacking. We are to "subdue" that which is causing such lack, and destruction. In other words, God expects His people to *"have dominion."* God put His earthly Kingdom in the hands of His family. It's not left to other people. The welfare of the nations is our concern.

We talking about ruling and reigning in this earth. It's takes both money and power to rule and reign. God will *"break in pieces"* the wealth and power of all the worldly kingdoms, and give it to His people. That is the purpose of the wealth transfer. However, wealth is only a tool. It is not our master. God is taking down the leaders of nations because they love money instead of people. They've sold their nations to the highest bidder, to heap up fortunes for themselves. Yes, they've heaped it up, but God's kids will put it on. We will use the wealth for the Kingdom and for the glory of our Heavenly Father. Okay. Let's continue with God's instructions for entering into our promise land. We are talking about the instructions God gave those He delivered out of Egypt. In these last days, we are also being delivered out of Egypt [the world system]. The instructions that applied to God's people back then, still apply to us today.

God told His people how to deal with the heathen [unbelievers] in the land. A heathen is anyone who is not in covenant with the True and Living God. We don't make covenants with the enemy. *"Thou shalt make no covenant with them, nor shew mercy unto them: neither shalt thou make marriages with them (Deuteronomy 7:2-3)."* God made it plain that His people are not to marry outside of their covenant. They were not to give their sons nor their daughters in marriage to the heathen. Why? *"For they will turn away thy son from following me, that they may serve other gods: so will the anger of the Lord be kindled against you, and destroy thee suddenly* (Deuteronomy 7:3-4)." When God spoke these words, the people had been in bondage for over four hundred years. They were slaves, which means that the people had been abused and misused by their masters, producing children with the enemy. How do we know? The Bible talks about a *"mixed"* multitude among God's people (Exodus 12:38). This word is used to describe the non-Hebrews among the slaves. Some were a *"mingled"* people by birth. Others were foreigners [Gentiles] who identified with God's people.

Consider what it's like for us today in America. Slaves were brought here from Africa and other nations. After four hundred years, the people are "mixed." Slave owners sired children by their slaves. It would be rare to find a "pure" offspring of those forefathers who came here as slaves all those years ago. Nevertheless, God instituted instructions after the people were released from slavery signifying that they were entering *"a new era."* They may have come out of bondage as a *"mixed multitude"* of former slaves and immigrants, Jews, Christians, Muslim, Agnostic, Atheist, but God is calling us all out of bondage as a *"holy nation;"* a people set aside for His glory. This is where we are today. God's people have been *"co-mingling"* with the Egyptians in thought, in deed, and in lifestyle. Many had no idea that they had been under the influence of the god of this world (II Corinthians 4:4). Even so, God established an order for His people. We must now commit to God's order in this New Kingdom Era that is before us.

The scripture also teaches us that before entering in their promise, the idols of the heathen must be removed from the land. *"But thus shall ye deal with them; ye shall destroy their altars, and break down their images, and cut down their groves, and burn their graven images with fire* (Deuteronomy 7:5)." If God's people are to inherit the land for the Kingdom, they must destroy the evil altars and burn the images of idols in the land. The Lord will instruct us to remove any relics or symbols that represent idols and burn them. What was once used for the praise of satanic worship must be dedicated back to Almighty God. Let us be reminded of what the Lord told Jeremiah. God put the man over nations and kingdoms for one purpose. *". . . to root out, and to pull down, and to destroy, and to throw down, to build, and to plant* (Jeremiah 1:9-10)." One must understand why God created the land in the first place. It was to build and plant what God desired in the earth. Mankind was created to be *"co-creators"* with God. Sin upset the plan for mankind, but just for a short season. Instead of doing the will of the Lord in *"a pristine, holy land,"* we have to do so in a land that is *"polluted"* with blood and every form of wickedness. Therefore, the land must be cleansed before planting what God desires. Every farmer knows that before you plant, the ground has to be tilled of weeds and stones, and everything that would prevent the seed from taking root. The same is true for God's Kingdom.

We are in the time of great harvest. God is giving us *"polluted"* cities and lands. *"And it shall be, when the LORD thy God shall have brought thee into the land which he sware unto thy fathers, to Abraham, to Isaac, and to Jacob, to give thee great and goodly cities, which thou buildedst not, And houses full of all good [things], which thou filledst not, and wells digged, which thou diggedst not, vineyards and olive trees, which thou plantedst not* (Deuteronomy 6:10-11)." This is covenant wealth that God swore to give Abraham and his seed. The wealth is the fulfillment of God's covenant. We cannot be covenanted with Almighty God and with the world at the same time. Therefore this wealth comes with a strong warning. *"Then beware lest thou forget the Lord, which brought thee forth out of the land of Egypt, from the house of bondage. Thou shalt fear the Lord thy God, and serve him, and shalt swear by his name. Ye shall not go after other gods, of the gods of the people which [are] round about you; (For the LORD thy God [is] a jealous God among you) lest the anger of the LORD thy God be kindled against thee, and destroy thee from off the face of the earth.* (Deuteronomy 6:12-15)."

Some might be bold enough to say, "Well, that was the Old Testament." Yes, it was. The times may have changed, but the purpose behind God's covenant has not. *"My covenant will I not break, nor alter the thing that is gone out of my lips* (Psalm 89:34)." Not only does God's covenant remain the same, so does the mandate for people. We are to take possession of the land for the Kingdom of God, not for ourselves, not for status in the world, but for the cause of Christ. This is about God's covenant promise to Abraham that he would be the *"heir of the world* (Romans 4:13)." This promise was not just for Abraham, but also for his seed, which we, the Church of Jesus Christ are his seed. The wealth transfer is about **"ownership"** of the world, as heirs of God and joint heirs with Jesus (Romans 8:17). Apostle Paul wrote those words to the Christians in Rome. He was speaking to Gentiles, or non-Jewish believers, about becoming heirs of God. The Jews already saw themselves as sons and heirs of God. Even so, God's promise of an inheritance was originally for the entire population of the earth. If sin had not occurred, the earth would have been inhabited by all the *"righteous"* sons and daughters of Adam. Sin upset the plan for mankind, but just for a short season. Therefore, God preached the message of His Blessing one family at a time, until Jesus came and opened up the gospel to the entire world.

God is recruiting sons and daughters for His Kingdom; kings and queens by right of salvation in the earth. We are more than conquerors through Him who loved us (Romans 8:37). We who have received the abundance of grace and the free gift of righteousness are called to *"reign in life,"* not by our own merits, but by what Jesus Christ had done (Romans 5:17). We are the kings of God's Kingdom. Jesus is the King of kings. We are lords of God's Kingdom. Jesus is the Lord of lords. We rule and reign by the commands of King Jesus. So, how does this work in the "real world?" To rule and reign in Christ, one must be able to see the world as God sees it; not with the physical senses, but with *"the eyes of the spirit."* The spirit realm is the real world. It's the realm that controls the world of the senses. Christians above all, should know this. The witches and occultist understand this reality. God also has a remnant who not only understand, but they also operate efficiently in the realm of the spirit as they perform the will of the Father. The Holy Spirit gave me a strong word a few years back about the person who would qualify to experience this end-time wealth and power transfer. Here is what He said. *"God has a people from every nation who will walk boldly in the promise of Abraham. They will rise up as* **"giants among men,"** *and run to the battle against the powers of darkness. When it is all said and done, they will be left standing, holding all the wealth and all the power of God's Kingdom, as rightful heirs of the Most High God. This will be the* **"New Breed"** *of leaders that Jesus is cultivating throughout the earth. They have been trained by the Holy Ghost* **"to hear what others cannot hear and see what others cannot see."** *Therefore they will be able to do what others could never do. These are little gods, who are walking in the power and boldness of their Father God. This is a powerful increase for mankind upon the earth. Ordinary men walking like gods in the earth?"*[5] This is a bold statement about men walking like gods in the earth, but this is exactly what the Lord shared with me. Religion taught us that salvation was about leaving this wicked world and going to Heaven. Not so! God saved us so that we could bring the will of Heaven down upon this wicked earth. *"Thy kingdom come. Thy will be done in earth, as [it is] in heaven* (Matthew 6:10)."

---

5   Matthews, Paula. "The Blessing Of Increase." *The War Journal (2011-2020) Volume III.* Atlanta: Spirit & Life Publications[SM], 2020. 125. Print.

Finally, I will share what the Lord told me about what is required before Jesus returns. He took me to Heaven and explained why we had to take back the earth. It was more about *"executing the judgment written."* This is also why we cannot afford to be covenanted with heathen. The Courts of Heaven have decreed the judgment and we the citizens of the Kingdom don't want to be found on the wrong side of that decree. God's Kingdom is advancing in the earth. Everything that is not aligned with Him will be shaken to the ground. Here is what the Lord shared with me about *His Kingdom Mission* for the earth.

The Lord took me to His *War Room*.[6] I recall walking into a rather large room with a large table in the center. On the surface of that table was a map of the world. The Lord said that this map represented the world under *"enemy occupation."* Then He showed me another map that was affixed to the wall. It was the *"legal document"* showing that the earth and its territories had been restored back to God. Everything was placed in *"receivership"* for the Body of Christ to claim and manage until Jesus returns. Here is the thing. According to the Lord, the Body of Christ must take possession of everything in that document, before Jesus can return. In my mind I was thinking "How can this be done?" Then I was drawn to take a closer look at that wall map. There were many family names on nations, cities and industries. Immediately I saw holdings with my name on them in various places in the world. The map reminded me of ancient Bible maps that showed how the land was divided among the Jewish tribes. It was then that it hit me! The Jews were not the only ones with a promised of land. God had land and property for all of His children. I saw it ever so clearly. There were businesses, inventions and innovations that donned the names of God's kids. Some of those things had not yet come down from Heaven, but they were on that map. The things I saw had to be re-possessed by specific members of the Body of Christ. I also saw proof in that *War Room* that Jesus cannot return until all things are restored back to God (Acts 3:21). This is a tall order for the Body of Christ. Nevertheless, this is the entire purpose of our existence in the earth, to prepare earth for the arrival of its Rightful King.

I had so many questions for the Lord. "How do I teach such a thing to people who are not expecting an inheritance in the land?" "What if people don't receive this message?" "What if they don't want to possess what is destined for their lives?" "How do you convince those who have been raised as

---

6 Matthews, Paula. "Recover All."*It's Time To Recover All!*. Atlanta: Spirit & Life Publications[SM], 2016. 20. Print.

slaves to accept their positions as kings of our God?" Nevertheless, God's plan is to transform us into a mighty nation, so that we can stand against our enemies, and rule in the Name of Jesus. This requires that we grow up spiritually. This also means putting on the whole armor of God. No king goes to war without suiting up. Neither should we, but go to war we must. The Bible indicates that there is a time *"when kings go forth to battle* (II Samuel 11:1)." We go to war because the Lord, our King has declared this as *"a time of war."* We will take back what belongs to God, and take it by force.

Indeed, this is a time of war (Ecclesiastes 3:8) for the Kingdom of God. Satan is battling the sons and daughters of God for our destiny. It's fight or die in the wilderness. However, we don't war with the weapons of man. The weapons of our warfare are not carnal, but they are mighty through God to pull down the strongholds of the enemy (II Corinthians 10:4). The strongholds are the *"fortified enemy positions"* which appear as thoughts and arguments that are against God. We battle against the spirit of antichrist which is working in our government, media and industry. They are proclaiming *"a perverted gospel."* God called this the voice of the *"false prophets"* of our day. The antichrist spirit is also working through the leaders of the Church. It is working through the leaders of nations. This is a spirit that exalts itself against the knowledge of Christ. However, God has given us powerful weapons to *"cast down"* all thoughts and imaginations that want to take preeminence over the word of God.

The Lord reigns over the heathen when the people of God are one with His will. Almighty God is our Protector and Defense. To think otherwise is absurd. Our faith is not in man. Our faith and hope is in our Creator God who chose us for His glory. Many have cursed themselves by turning away from God to honor men. We honor God first and foremost. Man cannot save us. According to the Lord, *"the works of man has ended."* That is the season in which we find ourselves. God says that *"it's time for the greater works to be done"* by His people. Who are we to argue with the Lord God Almighty? He is the Script Writer of our lives. He set the stage at creation and determined our habitation and existence before the foundation of the world. We know nothing without Him! Sure we are intelligent beings, but even that ability came from God, the Master Builder who created us. The creation can never be greater than the Creator. He created mankind as an extension, or subset of Himself. We learned in mathematics that the sum of the parts can never be greater than the whole. Nor can the subset of a thing be greater than the thing. So, why are the heathen raging? They rage and plot to kill for what they want because they have seen it work in times past. It just does not work against God's people in this season. To come against them is to come against God, Himself. So, why do the heathen continue to rage? It's the same answer to why sinners sin. That's just what heathens do.

God in Heaven is laughing at their futility. In the meantime, He is raising up His leaders in the earth. It shall be a **Battle Royale** as the kings of God's Kingdom make an open show of the kings of the earth. God is calling His people to *"rule"* in the midst of their enemies. Yet, we don't rule by our own power. Jesus is saying to us today, **"Rule and Reign in My Name!" "The Kingdom must be delivered up!"** I also heard the Spirit say, **"It's time to go possess the land!"**

We've heard the command. We have been given the Kingdom authority to take dominion in the earth for Jesus Christ, our Lord and King. Let us go up at once, and possess it; for we are well able to overcome it (Numbers 13:30)!

PRAYERS

For Deliverance

Are You Ready To Break
Those Evil Covenants And Curses
Off Your Life?

Then pray the following prayer:

Dear God,
I repent for making evil altars and following after idols and false gods of religion and the culture. I renounce every evil covenant that I made and that was made on my behalf, and that of my children, my business and anything that I possess or that is in my care. I decree with my mouth that those covenants with death are annulled and all agreements I made with hell shall not stand as I submit my allegiance to the Lordship of Jesus Christ.

Jesus, come into my heart. Cleanse me from every evil work that has come upon me, my family and all that I possess and care for. I want You to be my Lord and Savior. Fill me with Your Holy Spirit and lead me to your perfect path for my life. I pray this all in Jesus Name. Amen.

Enjoy you new found freedom in Christ!
If the Son therefore shall make you free, ye shall be free indeed.
John 8:36

For Salvation

Are You Ready To Reign Over The Circumstances Of Your Life?

The Bible says that they which receive abundance of grace and the gift of righteousness shall reign in life by one, Jesus Christ (Romans 5:17).

It begins when you **make Jesus the Lord of your life!**
Just read the following prayer aloud.

Dear God,

I want Jesus to be Lord over my life. I receive your free gift of righteousness right now. I renounce the devil and sin, and desire to spend the rest of my life serving you. Fill me with your Holy Spirit, and lead me to the your perfect will for my life. I want to receive an abundance of your grace to fulfill all you would require of me. I ask this all in Jesus' Name. Amen.

Welcome To The Family Of God!

You are now an heir of God, and a joint heir with Jesus, of everything that God possesses (Romans 8:17).

Read the Bible daily and ask the Holy Spirit to show you what is included in your inheritance. Then do whatever He tells you to do to obtain everything Jesus died, resurrected and ascended to give you. Join a spirit-filled Bible teaching church and enjoy your New Life In Christ!

For Dedication

Now That You Are Saved, Are You Ready To Possess The Land For God's Kingdom?

That means:
- Fasting and praying to get your Kingdom assignment.
- Preparing to go up against the giants in the land.
- Going in God's power and His timing, not your own.
- Having to slay your personal giants first.
- Laying down everything for the cause of Christ.
- Submitting to spiritual authority under the Holy Ghost

King Jesus,

I humbly submit myself for your Kingdom service. I begin by presenting my body as a living sacrifice, holy and acceptable to you. I also decree that I will no longer be conformed to the ways of this world. Instead, I promise to be transformed by the renewing of my mind to your will and your ways (Romans 12:1-2). I also submit myself under your chosen leadership and authority to learn what is necessary for your service. Teach me by Your Holy Spirit. Let the Spirit of the Lord be upon, as you anoint me to preach the gospel to the poor; and send me to heal the brokenhearted, to preach deliverance to the captives, and recovering of sight to the blind, to set at liberty them that are bruised (Luke 4:18). I submit myself to you, Jesus to proclaim the acceptable year of the LORD, and the day of Vengeance of our God; to comfort all that mourn (Isaiah 61:2). Knowing that greater is He that is in me, than he that is in this world (I John 4:4). And, as You are, so are we in this world (I John 4:17).

Now, Lord Jesus, Anoint me, Teach and Guide me, to be your lawful and faithful Kingdom servant. Here I am, Lord, send me!

www.ingramcontent.com/pod-product-compliance
Lightning Source LLC
Chambersburg PA
CBHW071848230426
43671CB00012B/2110